W9-CHQ-761

Johns Hopkins University

Baltimore, Maryland

Written by Christina Pommer

Edited by Adam Burns, Kristen Burns, Meghan Dowdell, and Jon Skindzier

Layout by Alyson Pope

Additional contributions by Omid Gohari, Christina Koshzow, Chris Mason, Joey Rahimi, and Luke Skurman

ISBN # 1-4274-0082-2
ISSN # 1551-9392
© Copyright 2006 College Prowler
All Rights Reserved
Printed in the U.S.A.
www.collegeprowler.com

Last updated 4/18/08

Special Thanks To: Babs Carryer, Andy Hannah, LaunchCyte, Tim O'Brien, Bob Sehlinger, Thomas Emerson, Andrew Skurman, Barbara Skurman, Bert Mann, Dave Lehman, Daniel Fayock, Chris Babyak, The Donald H. Jones Center for Entrepreneurship, Terry Slease, Jerry McGinnis, Bill Ecenberger, Idie McGinty, Kyle Russell, Jacque Zaremba, Larry Winderbaum, Roland Allen, Jon Reider, Team Evankovich, Lauren Varacalli, Abu Noaman, Mark Exler, Daniel Steinmeyer, Jared Cohon, Gabriela Oates, David Koegler, and Glen Meakem, and the Johns Hopkins University Bounce-Back Team.

College Prowler®
5001 Baum Blvd.
Suite 750
Pittsburgh, PA 15213

Phone: 1-800-290-2682
Fax: 1-800-772-4972
E-Mail: info@collegeprowler.com
Web Site: www.collegeprowler.com

How this all started...

When I was trying to find the perfect college, I used every resource that was available to me. I went online to visit school websites; I talked with my high school guidance counselor; I read book after book; I hired a private counselor. Sure, this was all very helpful, but nothing really told me what life was like at the schools I cared about. These sources weren't giving me enough information to be totally confident in my decision.

In all my research, there were only two ways to get the information I wanted.

The first was to physically visit the campuses and see if things were really how the brochures described them, but this was quite expensive and not always feasible. The second involved a missing ingredient: the students. Actually talking to a few students at those schools gave me a taste of the information that I needed so badly. The problem was that I wanted more but didn't have access to enough people.

In the end, I weighed my options and decided on a school that felt right and had a great academic reputation, but truth be told, the choice was still very much a crapshoot. I had done as much research as any other student, but was I 100 percent positive that I had picked the school of my dreams?

Absolutely not.

My dream in creating *College Prowler* was to build a resource that people can use with confidence. My own college search experience taught me the importance of gaining true insider insight; that's why the majority of this guide is composed of quotes from actual students. After all, shouldn't you hear about a school from the people who know it best?

I hope you enjoy reading this book as much as I've enjoyed putting it together. Tell me what you think when you get a chance. I'd love to hear your college selection stories.

Luke Skurman
CEO and Co-Founder
lukeskurman@collegeprowler.com

Welcome to College Prowler®

During the writing of College Prowler's guidebooks, we felt it was critical that our content was unbiased and unaffiliated with any college or university. We think it's important that our readers get honest information and a realistic impression of the student opinions on any campus—that's why if any aspect of a particular school is terrible, we (unlike a campus brochure) intend to publish it. While we do keep an eye out for the occasional extremist—the cheerleader or the cynic—we take pride in letting the students tell it like it is. We strive to create a book that's as representative as possible of each particular campus. Our books cover both the good and the bad, and whether the survey responses point to recurring trends or a variation in opinion, these sentiments are directly and proportionally expressed through our guides.

College Prowler guidebooks are in the hands of students throughout the entire process of their creation. Because you can't make student-written guides without the students, we have students at each campus who help write, randomly survey their peers, edit, layout, and perform accuracy checks on every book that we publish. From the very beginning, student writers gather the most up-to-date stats, facts, and inside information on their colleges. They fill each section with student quotes and summarize the findings in editorial reviews. In addition, each school receives a collection of letter grades (A through F) that reflect student opinion and help to represent contentment, prominence, or satisfaction for each of our 20 specific categories. Just as in grade school, the higher the mark the more content, more prominent, or more satisfied the students are with the particular category.

Once a book is written, additional students serve as editors and check for accuracy even more extensively. Our bounce-back team—a group of randomly selected students who have no involvement with the project—are asked to read over the material in order to help ensure that the book accurately expresses every aspect of the university and its students. This same process is applied to the 200-plus schools College Prowler currently covers. Each book is the result of endless student contributions, hundreds of pages of research and writing, and countless hours of hard work. All of this has led to the creation of a student information network that stretches across the nation to every school that we cover. It's no easy accomplishment, but it's the reason that our guides are such a great resource.

When reading our books and looking at our grades, keep in mind that every college is different and that the students who make up each school are not uniform—as a result, it is important to assess schools on a case-by-case basis. Because it's impossible to summarize an entire school with a single number or description, each book provides a dialogue, not a decision, that's made up of 20 different topics and hundreds of student quotes. In the end, we hope that this guide will serve as a valuable tool in your college selection process. Enjoy!

OMID GOHARI ○ CHRISTINA KOSHZOW ○ CHRIS MASON ○ JOEY RAHIMI ○ LUKE SKURMAN ○
The College Prowler Team

Table of Contents

Introduction from the Author

When you tell people that you're looking at/applying to/attending Johns Hopkins, be prepared for one response. "So, you want to be a doctor?" Actually, only one-third of Hopkins undergrads are pre-meds, but the television show "Hopkins 24" didn't do much to change the perception that Hopkins has one of the best medical programs in the world. Hopkins, however, also has great, although lesser known, programs in many other subjects. The biomedical engineering major is number one in the country, and the writing seminars, classics, and computer science programs are all excellent, as well. There is no major at Johns Hopkins where students who work hard won't get a great education. If you want to complement your major with research, Hopkins is the place for you. Professors encourage independent studies and lab work in the humanities, natural sciences, and engineering. Students don't complain about the quality of academics at Hopkins.

Freshmen and sophomores are required to live on campus, and over 99% of all juniors and seniors live within a 10-minute walk of the Homewood campus. Student life is improving each year. One of the graduating classes a few years back donated money for future classes' social events, and the class of 2003 donated money to renovate Levering Hall into a proper student union. There are hundreds of student-run organizations, enough to match any interest, from sports to community service to performing arts. Hopkins also hosts numerous academic lectures each week, bringing in speakers from around the world. Although some students complain about the lack of social life at Hopkins, there is a lot to do outside of class if you stop studying and look around.

I wish you luck in looking for a university where you can balance academics and social activities. It's difficult to gauge where you'll fit in just by looking at college statistics in a guidebook. Hopefully, the students' quotations in this guidebook will help you determine if Hopkins seems like a good match for you. There's a good chance that it might fit if you're a serious student who enjoys being challenged by academics and is able to create your own social life. If you're seriously considering attending Hopkins, I'd encourage you to visit and stay overnight, if at all possible. Good luck in your search.

Christina Pommer, Author
Johns Hopkins University

By the Numbers

General Information

Johns Hopkins
3400 North Charles St.
Baltimore, MD 21218

Control:
Private

Academic Calendar:
4-1-4

Religious Affiliation:
None

Founded:
1876

Web Site:
www.jhu.edu

Main Phone:
(410) 516-8000

Student Body

**Full-Time
Undergraduates:**
4,412

**Part-Time
Undergraduates:**
59

**Full-Time Male
Undergraduates:**
2,370

**Full-Time Female
Undergraduates:**
2,101

Admissions

Overall Acceptance Rate:
27%

Total Applicants:
13,900

Total Acceptances:
3,726

Freshman Enrollment:
1,207

Yield (% of admitted students who actually enroll):
32%

Early Decision Available?
Yes

Early Action Available?
No

Early Decision Deadline:
November 1

Early Decision Notification:
December 15

Regular Decision Deadline:
January 1

Regular Decision Notification:
April 1

Must-Reply-By Date:
May 1

Applicants Placed on Waiting List:
2,618

Applicants Accepting Place on Waiting List:
1,258

Students Enrolled from Waiting List:
1

Transfer Applications Received:
658

Transfer Students Accepted:
99

Transfer Students Enrolled:
36

Transfer Acceptance Rate:
15%

Common Application Accepted?
Yes

Supplemental Forms?
Required

Admissions E-Mail: gotojhu@jhu.edu

Admissions Web Site:
webapps.jhu.edu/jhuniverse/admissions

Freshman Retention Rate:
97%

SAT I or ACT Required?
Yes, either may be used

➜

**SAT I Range
(25th–75th Percentile):**
1290–1490

**SAT I Verbal Range
(25th–75th Percentile):**
630–730

**SAT I Math Range
(25th–75th Percentile):**
660–760

**Top 10% of High
School Class:**
75%

Application Fee:
$70

SAT II Requirements:
Required only if ACT is not taken. You must take three SAT II tests, one of which must be writing. The other two should be related to your discipline.

Financial Information

Full-Time Tuition:
$35,900

Room and Board:
$11,092

Books and Supplies:
$1,000

**Average Need-Based
Financial Aid Package
(including loans, work-
study, and other sources):**
$29,303

**Students Who Applied
for Financial Aid:**
55%

**Applicants Who
Received Aid:**
81%

**Financial Aid
Forms Deadline:**
March 1

Financial Aid Phone:
(410) 516-8028

Financial Aid E-Mail:
fin_aid@jhu.edu

Academics

The Lowdown On...
Academics

Degrees Awarded:
Bachelor's
Master's
Doctoral

Most Popular Majors:
12% International relations and affairs

9% Biomedical/medical engineering

7% Economics

6% Computer and information sciences

6% Psychology

Undergraduate Schools:
Krieger School of Arts and Sciences
Peabody Institute
School of Education
School of Nursing
Whiting School of Engineering

Full-Time Faculty:
3,421

Faculty with Terminal Degree:	Average Course Load:
92%	15–18 credit hours per semester

Student-to-Faculty Ratio:
10:1

Graduation Rates:
Four-Year: 83%
Five-Year: 91%
Six-Year: 93%

Special Degree Options

Dual-degree within School of Arts and Sciences, School of Engineering, and Peabody Conservatory of Music; Five-Year bachelors/masters program in international studies; accelerated masters program by permission of department

AP Test Score Requirements

Possible credit for scores of four or five for biology (five only), chemistry, computer science A/B, french language, German language, macroeconomics (five only, with instructor's permission), mathematics calculus A/B, mathematics calculus B/C (score of three equal A/B test score of five, and a score of four or five tests you out of two classes), microeconomics (five only, with instructor's permission), physic C first part, physics C second part (score of four or five for either), Spanish language, and statistics

IB Test Score Requirements

Possible credit for scores of six or seven for biology (only seven), chemistry, computer science, French, German, math, math with further math, physics (score of six gets credit for one class, score of seven gets credit for two classes), Spanish

Did You Know?

 Johns Hopkins follows **a different class schedule** from many other universities. Classes that meet more than once a week meet for 50 minutes Monday, Tuesday, and Wednesday, or for 75 minutes Thursday and Friday.

Many introductory courses are taught in large lecture halls. Graduate teaching assistants lead sections once a week. These sections are **discussion based, and only 15 students are allowed in each**.

During Intersession (which occurs the last three weeks in January), Hopkins offers a mix of academic and entertaining classes, (such as **wine tasting, massage, and dance**). There are also several educational trips offered. In the past, students have traveled to Ghana and the Galapagos Islands.

Sample Academic Clubs
Association for Computing Machinery, College Bowl, JHU Academic Bowl, National Society of Collegiate Scholars, Math Club, Pre-Law Society, Public Health Students' Forum

Best Places to Study
HUT library, MSE library, AMR I study lounge, Bloomberg mezzanine

Students Speak Out On...
Academics

"Because JHU is a research university, and many of the professors are high profile, you are less likely to receive personal attention. You are often really on your own."

Q "Despite its reputation as being cut-throat, in most subjects, there's a lot of teamwork. **Students who do best usually work together**, especially in math and physics. Most of the teachers seem to care about how students do and are accessible, but in some cases, I feel like they don't realize how lucky they are to have the students they do. They need to teach at a community college to realize what it's like to teach students who really don't care about class."

Q "**Academics at Hopkins are some of the best anywhere**, but some of the professors know that they are working at the forefront of their fields and only want to teach upperclass students within their field of expertise. It can be hard to find lower-level courses that you can take (and understand) simply because you wanted to learn about a subject. You have to take four courses that are completely outside your major, but most students don't branch out too much other than that."

Q "The teachers are all different. Some are really enthusiastic and interested, while others aren't. **You can add and drop classes within the first couple weeks**, though, which gives you time to see if you like the professor or not. Most teachers are a lot more friendly and helpful if you see them outside of class. They really like it when you come to their office hours."

Q "Generally, Hopkins professors are very knowledgeable in their subjects. **Large lecture courses are likely to be a little impersonal**. How many of these one takes depends on his major. Humanities classes tend to be smaller seminars."

Q "Professors are nice and very intelligent. They are definitely hard and expect a lot from their students. Most of them genuinely care about the students and will challenge your mind! Most of my classes were big freshman year because I was taking all the preliminary pre-med classes. I didn't get as much of a chance to meet my teachers. However, **by sophomore year, classes are all relatively small**. All professors have scheduled office hours, and they will meet with you any other time if you e-mail them."

Q "**The professors here absolutely are amazing**. I haven't encountered a single one I haven't liked as a professor or as a person."

Q "The teachers are good, although your first year, you'll **spend most of your one-on-one non-lecture time with TAs** (although not true of all classes). My experience with TAs has been wonderful, and I really like the idea of a lecture with the professor and a section with a TA. Teaching assistants are grad students, and I feel more comfortable in a setting with people closer in age. It can be a bit daunting to deal with someone who is the top in their field. Still, many of the professors are very approachable, and there are many smaller classes taught only by professors."

Q "Many of **the teachers really don't care if you like them**. They don't care if you understand the material, and they don't care if their class is interesting."

Q "**Teachers are always accessible** and hold office hours every week. Sometimes, they bribe us to come visit with anything from cookies to bringing their dogs. My experience is mostly with the psychology department, and all the professors I've had in those classes have been excellent."

Q "There are some really good teachers—especially the business teachers. But then there are some poor teachers who focus only on their research. It is a main focal point at Hopkins, and **the University brings in some of the best** people in the world in their fields."

Q "The teachers seem to be pretty good lecturers. Some make nasty, hard exams just for kicks; others put their class on a C- curve for fun. I don't really worry about it, but grades are definitely lower here than at the Ivies. It doesn't really hurt as long as you're being pulled down at the top, because **grad schools know how hard they grade at Hopkins**."

Q "I have enjoyed learning from the professors at Hopkins. Although they are all busy, I have found that **they are genuinely interested in helping students learn**. If students make an effort to go to office hours, they should have no complaints with professors."

The College Prowler Take On...
Academics

Hopkins students are generally pleased with academics. If you ask many students the deciding factor in choosing to attend Hopkins, academics tops the list of reasons. There is some contention between engineering/science and humanities/social science students. The latter have more control over their schedules, and their classes focus less on memorization and more on critical thinking. Students also disagree on the quality of teaching. In large lecture courses, professors don't really get a chance to get to know the students, while in upper-level courses, most make the effort, although some are more interested in their own research. However, there is a consensus that almost all teachers appreciate it when students attend their office hours. In courses with teaching assistants, they are often more accessible than professors and more interested in helping students learn.

Academics at Hopkins would be stronger if there were greater camaraderie and individual attention in lower-level lecture courses. Students who need or want a lot of individual attention have to make the effort to meet the professor or teaching assistant outside of class. This is less true in small, upper-level seminar courses. Students also complain about the lack of grade inflation at Hopkins, which puts them at a disadvantage when compared with student's attending other top universities. Even with lower grades, students at Hopkins have access to some of the best professors and researchers in the world. Hopkins provides ample opportunities for students to design independent studies and research, as well as encouraging them to take at least a few classes outside their major.

The College Prowler® Grade on
Academics: A-

A high Academics grade generally indicates that professors are knowledgeable, accessible, and genuinely interested in their students' welfare. Other determining factors include class size, how well professors communicate, and whether or not classes are engaging.

Local Atmosphere

The Lowdown On...
Local Atmosphere

Region:
Mid Atlantic

City, State:
Baltimore, MD

Setting:
Urban

Distance from Washington DC:
45 miles

Distance from Philadelphia:
100 miles

Points of Interest:
American Dime Museum
B and O Railroad Museum
Babe Ruth Museum
Baltimore Museum of Art
Edgar Allan Poe House
Fell's Point
Museum of Industry
Fort McHenry

(Points of Interest, continued)

Homewood and
Evergreen Houses

Inner Harbor

Lacrosse Museum

Lexington Market

Maryland Science Center

Museum of Dentistry

National Aquarium

Star Spangled Banner House

Walter's Art Gallery

Closest Shopping Malls or Plazas:

Arundel Mills
7000 Arundel Mills Cir.
Hanover, MD
(410) 540-5100

Harbor Place and the Gallery
200 East Pratt St.
Baltimore, MD
(410) 332-4191

Owings Mills Town Center
10300 Owings Mills Blvd.
Owings Mills, MD
(410) 363-7000

Towson Town Center
825 Dulaney Rd.
Towson, MD
(410) 494-8800

Closest Movie Theaters:

AMC Towson Commons 8
York Rd. and Pennsylvania Ave.
Towson, MD 21204
(410) 825-5233

Charles Theatre
1711 North Charles St.
Baltimore, MD 21201
(410) 727-3456

Loews White Marsh 16
White Marsh Blvd. at I-95
White Marsh, MD 21162
(410) 933-9034

Muvico Egyptian 24
7000 Arundel Mills Cir., C-1
Hanover, MD 21076
(443) 755-8992

Senator Theatre
5904 York Rd.
Baltimore, MD 21212
(410) 435-8338

Major Sports Teams:

Baltimore Orioles (baseball)

Baltimore Ravens (football)

City Web Sites

www.baltimore.org

www.baltimoretourism.com

Did You Know?

5 Fun Facts about Baltimore:

- **A Baltimore pharmacist created Noxzema** somewhat by accident in the early 1900s.

- **Little Italy** holds free outdoor movie nights on Fridays during the summer.

- **Edgar Allen Poe** spent a great deal of his life and died in Baltimore; the Raven football team is a tribute to his well-known poem "The Raven." Plus, the three team mascots are all ravens named Edgar, Allen, and Poe.

- Baltimore used to have the motto, "**The city that reads**," but the mayor changed it to "The Greatest City in America" hoping it would inspire citizens to think more highly of the city.

- John Waters uses **working-class Baltimore** (Hamden) as the setting for his films, which include *Pecker*, *Pink Flamingos*, and *Hairspray*.

Famous People from Baltimore:

Jimmy's Chicken Shack – Rock musicians

Dru Hill – R&B group

H.L. Menken – Writer

Edgar Allan Poe – Writer (actually, he just died in Baltimore, but Baltimore has claimed him as its own)

Cal Ripkin, Jr. – Baseball great

Babe Ruth – Baseball great

John Waters – Filmmaker

Local Slang:

Bawlmer – Baltimore

Duckpin bowling – Like 10-pin bowling, but a lot smaller

Hon – Term of endearment or recognition. Example: "Here you go, hon."

Students Speak Out On...
Local Atmosphere

"Visit the Inner Harbor. There are lots of places to go there, like the National Aquarium, ESPN Zone, Hard Rock Café, the Cheesecake Factory, and Legal Sea Foods. You can rent paddle boats there and see street performers."

Q "One of the advantages of Hopkins's location in Baltimore is that there are tons of festivals, and **the city has a really unique atmosphere—from the accent to beehive hairdos**. Students who don't have cars complain a lot more than those who do. It's not really safe to walk places because a lot of things are separated by bad neighborhoods. The more people actually explore Baltimore, the more they seem to like it. The city has charm, but it's hidden. One example is Sherwood Gardens, a quaint park near Hopkins that's surrounded by mansions. Students call it the "tulip garden" because of all the flowers, but most don't know it's maintained by a Hopkins physics professor."

Q "I grew up near Baltimore, so I'm biased about the city. I think it's great, but a lot of students really don't like it here. They complain that there's nothing to do, but it's not true. There's not always a whole lot to do right around Hopkins, and there isn't really a city center (other than the Harbor, which is geared to tourists), but there are lots of neighborhoods. They have restaurants and bars. Also, many students don't know that **there are several wineries outside Baltimore that host weekly events**. I would suggest Hamden (famous for John Water's movies), Mount Vernon for bars and ethnic restaurants, and Annapolis, Harper's Ferry, or Washington DC for a day away from Baltimore."

Q "There are several other colleges in Baltimore, which is nice because **Hopkins really isn't big enough to support a college atmosphere in the city on its own**. Some parts of Baltimore are kind of unsavory, although it's been improving greatly in the past few years. Generally, it's good to be careful. Hopkins has an excellent shuttle service, which is a great way to get around the immediate area. As far as things to visit, DC is just a stone's throw away, and there are a number of options there. Baltimore itself has the things you'd expect from a city of its size (a zoo, sporting events, museums), and some unique stuff, too. See the aquarium at least once."

Q "I have few complaints about Baltimore. **I feel like Hopkins is a rather sheltered environment**. Due to lack of convenient transportation, I do not get off campus often. Other universities are present, but I have yet to have a reason to go to another campus. Some places to visit are the Lyric Opera House, Inner Harbor, and Towson Mall."

Q "**The atmosphere is okay**. There isn't that much to do in Baltimore really, other than clubs and the usual. The Baltimore Museum of Art is right next to campus, but it's not that great of an art museum. I like the aquarium."

Q "There are **three other universities down the street from Hopkins: Loyola, Towson University, and Goucher**. I have a couple friends at Loyola, and it's not hard to get there. The atmosphere is very suburban right around the school, and more city-like towards Mount Vernon and the Harbor. Stay away from Greenmount Street and the ghetto-like area opposite of Towson. Definitely visit the Harbor and Fell's Point."

Q "There are other universities where we party, especially Towson and Loyola. I like to go to Baltimore's Inner Harbor, and DC is easily accessible from here. **Baltimore has a great symphony orchestra and a nice opera house**. Also, the Charles Village area around campus is nice."

Q "Directly around us are a few restaurants and a supermarket. Just a taxi ride away is the Inner Harbor, which has an aquarium, Hard Rock Café, ESPN Zone, a science center, and few shopping malls. There are a few other colleges in the area. **There is also a shuttle to a large mall 30 minutes away and a movie theater**."

Q "It's Baltimore. You can visit the Inner Harbor or the mall in Towson, but there isn't always a lot to do. **Most people hang around campus** until they get a better feel for the place. There are a lot of colleges around, though, and they mostly come to JHU because we are one of the only colleges in the area that has frats."

Q "The area right around Hopkins is geared towards the school, with coffee shops and cafés. **The Baltimore Museum of Art is next door**, which is great to just walk around on a day off. Towson University, Notre Dame of MD, and Loyola are nearby colleges."

Q "There are at least five or six universities around or in Baltimore, and they're easy to get to by shuttle. Definitely visit Inner Harbor (good food in tourist area), Fell's Point (bars and shopping), and Little Italy (good food). **Stay away from the ghetto areas**."

Q "As far our location, **we seem to be on the border between both nice and not-so-nice areas**. If you go in the direction of south, you will possibly encounter dangerous areas, while north leads to nicer areas, (but it is still not completely safe late at night). The harbor is a popular place, too, because it has lots of restaurants, clubs, the Aquarium, and plenty of other stuff to do."

Q "The three other schools near Hopkins come down for parties all the time, and we go there a bit, as well. There's a ton to do in Baltimore, but **I don't get a chance to go site-seeing that much**. DC is also really close by, and it's only five dollars on weekdays to get there."

The College Prowler Take On...
Local Atmosphere

Baltimore is a city that takes time to love. It also might take a car and a friend who knows the way around. Baltimore is a city of neighborhoods, and each of these has a very distinctive feel. Johns Hopkins straddles several neighborhoods: Roland Park, a residential neighborhood with parks and mansions; Charles Village, a collegiate-urban environment; and Hamden, a working-class neighborhood that, with John Waters's help, just realized the marketability of its kitschiness. A little further from campus, Mount Vernon houses Peabody Conservatory, Maryland Institute College of Art, and several theaters. It is known for being a trendy artists' area. Baltimore does not have a city center where residents hang out. From early spring through fall, neighborhoods host festivals that celebrate the particular feel of their neighborhoods with food, vendors, and games. However, students who don't read city papers often don't know about neighborhood events, and students without cars have no ways to attend them. Freshmen mainly go to the mall in Towson and the Inner Harbor, both of which can get old quickly. As several students stated, though, make sure you visit the National Aquarium at least once.

Baltimore is a good medium-sized city. Those who come from big cities are disappointed by the lack of activities, but there are a number of activities for a city of its size, even though many are not publicized well. Keep in mind that it is within four hours of Washington DC, Ocean City, Richmond, Philadelphia, Pittsburgh, Newark, and New York City.

B+

The College Prowler® Grade on

Local Atmosphere: B+

A high Local Atmosphere grade indicates that the area surrounding campus is safe and scenic. Other factors include nearby attractions, proximity to other schools, and the town's attitude toward students.

Safety & Security

The Lowdown On...
Safety & Security

Number of JHU Police:
60

JHU Police Phone:
(410) 516-7777

Safety Services:
Emergency vans
Publication of all crimes occurring on or near campus
Security escort vans
Self defense classes
Walking escorts and monitors

Health Services:
Basic medical services
Counseling and psychological services
HERO emergency response unit
On-site pharmaceuticals
STD screening

Health Center Office Hours:
Monday–Friday 8:30 a.m.–5 p.m. (closed 11 a.m.–1 p.m. Wednesday),
Saturday 9 a.m.–12 p.m.

Did You Know?

Hop Cops are notorious for handing out "rape whistles" during orientation. Students are encouraged to carry these **glow-in-the-dark whistles** with them all the time. If students ever get in trouble, they can blow the whistle to draw attention to themselves and their attacker.

Hopkins Emergency Response Organization (HERO) is staffed by students who pass a rigorous course and exam. They are trained to respond in emergency situations. You can identify them around campus by their big blue backpacks.

Hopkins Security publishes all of the school's crime statistics. Students who are interested can go to the office in Shriver Hall to find information on all recent cases. The office also keeps **a map that color codes crimes**. It is easy to look at this map and find crime statistics from the past year for any area within a mile of campus.

Students Speak Out On...
Safety & Security

"Security is quite good. Most of the Hop Cops are retired police officers. They're very capable and pretty friendly."

Q "The campus itself is pretty safe, but **as soon as you're two blocks away, watch your back or go with a friend**. The best thing about security on campus is that the guards are friendly and nice to talk with late at night. One particular late-night guard in Wolman is known as 'Momma,' and students frequently come by to chat or play cards with her."

Q "The campus feels safe. **There are Hop Cops everywhere**. ResLife always tells students to lock doors in their dorms, but most don't. I've only heard of a few burglaries on campus over the past four years. Off campus, there is still Hop Cop and Baltimore police presence, but not as much as on campus. The Roland Park area is pretty nice and safe, but you still shouldn't forget that the school's right in the middle of the city."

Q "**I always feel safe** on campus."

Q "Off campus isn't exactly the safest area of the country. **Don't go anywhere at night without someone else**, but during the day, you'll probably be fine. On campus is definitely pretty safe. There are security guards on patrol called Hop Cops."

Q "I've never had any problems, but I'm a guy. **We walk our female friends home at night** from wherever we've been hanging out—not because of any real perceived need, but because it just makes safety sense in an urban area."

Q "Security and safety on campus is very good. Off campus, though, there have been several armed robberies a few blocks from campus. However, if you travel in a group at night and utilize the security shuttles, which will drop you off anywhere within a one mile radius, you should be fine. I've never had any problems with crime. The biggest problem is when you live off campus junior and senior year because **you don't have the on-campus security**."

Q "**We have Hopkins police patrolling the campus at all hours**. There are emergency phones throughout campus that respond immediately when they are pressed. Four of the dorms are accessible with access cards and keys to the rooms, and security guards sit at the front desks of two of them. The other two dorms are accessible only with keys. But other than that, I have never felt a safety issue at Hopkins. I live in a very safe suburb, and I feel just as safe at school as I feel at home. Our campus is very enclosed, and you don't notice strange characters walking around or feel unsafe at all. Of course, you have to be smart. Don't walk around by yourself off campus at night or wander too far."

Q "Although Hopkins is not in the best part of Baltimore, **campus security is superb**. There are Hop Cops located at every building, and many of them roam the campus, as well. I have never felt in danger on the campus, however, you shouldn't walk across campus or on the streets alone at night. The Hop Cops are awesome and will help you with anything."

Q "Security and safety on campus are pretty good. **There are emergency phones pretty much everywhere** in sight, and there are always Hop Cops walking. I wouldn't suggest going anywhere alone or even with two or three people. There are even parts of the city that I wouldn't visit at all under any circumstances."

Q "We do have crime, and there are definitely **neighborhoods all Hopkins students know not to venture into**—on foot or alone. I've never felt uncomfortable around or on campus and have always felt safe and secure. It's simply a matter of being smart in a city. Out of all Hopkins students, 99.9 percent get through college never seeing a crime, and the .1 percent who do usually have done something not so smart to put themselves in a dangerous situation."

Q "The campus is pretty safe. I feel safe walking around at night alone, but my friends always yell at me for it. However, **off campus is not safe**. Hopkins is described as an island in Baltimore. For that reason, few freshmen travel far from the campus."

Q "**Security and safety on campus is excellent**. I always feel very safe, even when returning to my dorm alone at odd hours of the night. Although the campus itself is very safe, the surrounding areas are a little sketchy. During orientation, student advisors will tell you about places that aren't too safe—not that you'd ever want to go there anyway. These not-so-safe places are a few blocks from the school; the area adjacent to the school is just fine."

The College Prowler Take On...
Safety & Security

Hopkins has great security on campus. The presence of Hop Cops and other security guards 24 hours a day allows students to walk around campus safely. In addition, the security office runs both walking and driving escort services to take students where they want to go within a mile of campus. There is never an excuse for walking alone after dark. When students leave campus, they need to remember that they live in a city. They should remain aware of their surroundings and avoid traveling alone. Some streets near campus are not safe, but the University offers precautions so that students remain safe.

Hopkins has worked very diligently to make sure that the campus is safe for students. The escort service, emergency phones, and police presence are services the school offers to keep its students safe within the confines of the campus. Crime on campus is almost nonexistent. There are cases of crime several blocks from the campus—mostly crimes against property—but the school does everything it can do to eliminate this. Hop Cops even patrol areas of high student traffic that are located off campus to discourage crime. If students follow security guidelines, it is unlikely that they will be victims of crime.

B-

The College Prowler® Grade on

Safety & Security: B-

A high grade in Safety & Security means that students generally feel safe, campus police are visible, blue-light phones and escort services are readily available, and safety precautions are not overly necessary.

Computers

The Lowdown On...
Computers

High-Speed Network?
Yes

Wireless Network?
Yes

Number of Labs:
4

Number of Computers:
460

Operating Systems:
Mac, Windows

Free Software

None

24-Hour Labs

Yes, HAC Lab (closes on weekend nights), Wolman (only open to those who live in Wolman and McCoy)

Charge to Print?

Twenty-five cents for color copies, five cents for black copies in the HAC Lab, and two cent for copies in the residential labs

Did You Know?

The Digital Media Center contains 12 Dell and Apple computers with software for digital video editing, video transitions/effects, vector graphics, Web site creation, animation, photo and image manipulation, 3-D modeling, and virtual drawing and painting. The Center offers approximately **30 free classes to students**, including classes in animation concepts, digital photography, video editing, and digital audio. Students can also rent video cameras, light and sound equipment, and cables. The Web site of the Digital Media Center is *http://digitalmedia.jhu.edu/Main/Home.cfm*.

Students Speak Out On...
Computers

> "The computer lab is available 24/7, and there are computers in the library. However, IM is frequently used as communication, so I'd recommend bringing one anyway."

Q "I've never had any trouble with the network. I didn't have a computer when I arrived and I could do all my work, but it's a lot more convenient to have your own computer. You also have to beware of the computers in the labs corrupting your disks. **Back everything up on the computers** because lots of people will tell you about times they've lost their files."

Q "The dorms' **Ethernet access is definitely worth it**. I never had much occasion to use the computer labs until I moved off campus. I've found them to be pretty good, though, they do get a bit crowded towards the end of the semester."

Q "Having a personal computer is not necessary. Computer labs are **generally crowded in the evenings**, but Internet access is fast."

Q "You should bring a computer for Instant Messenger (IM) and downloading stuff because the network's extremely good. But, **the computer labs aren't that crowded**. You can rack up some pretty large printing bills if you always use the school's labs."

Q "Bring your own computer, but **Hopkins remains very up-to-date with their computers labs**. The school recently purchased 50-plus Dell 1.8 ghz machines."

Q "We use Ethernet, which is an incredibly fast connection. All rooms are set up for this system, and you get an Internet cord when you come to Hopkins. **Most students do have their own computer, but it isn't necessary**. We have a HAC lab, which is open 24/7 and has every computer resource you could need—scanners, printers, PCs. There are also other computer labs in the dorms that are open at certain hours in the afternoon. They are convenient for printing out long readings for class, and are rarely, if ever, crowded."

Q "**The labs aren't crowded but are inaccessible**. The library computers don't have word processors because they don't want students using them all the time. I would suggest bringing your own computer—preferably a laptop because you can take it to class, outside, or to the study lounge."

Q "The **network is very fast**, although recently they have started blocking 'illegal' file-sharing utilities like Kazaa and Morpheus. It's a drag, but there are always other ways to get music."

Q "Bring your own computer. **The labs are pretty crowded around finals time**, although I've never had a hard time finding a computer. It's more annoying to have to trek somewhere when you want to type something at an odd hour. Also, IM is the number-one means of communication at Hopkins—it's invaluable. I'm always using it to plan to meet up with friends, or to see what they are up to."

Q "Many students like laptops so they can take it to the library and do work there, or just to sit on the 'beach' and write essays. While labs can become busy at the end of the semester, **I don't think I've ever had a problem finding a computer** to use when I needed one."

The College Prowler Take On...
Computers

The computer network is fast and reliable. Most students bring their own computers and don't rely on the computer labs. They will freely admit, however, that they recommend bringing your own computer primarily due to convenience. Instant Messenger is one of the main ways that students communicate with each other, and illegal file-sharing is rampant (even though the Hopkins administration has been increasing security within the Hopkins network to discourage this behavior). In addition, there is only one computer lab that is open 24 hours a day. Many students like to be free to work in places other than a computer lab. Students also think that printing is expensive at this lab, but both PCs and Macs are almost always available. The other labs are open only at certain times throughout the day. In these labs, no one is available to help if you have problems. Printing is cheap, but unreliable. If you don't bring a computer, you won't have any problem getting work done, but you may feel left out since you will be in the minority.

The computer network is entirely adequate for a school of Hopkins's size. The Ethernet connection is fast and doesn't slow down when many students are online. The main computer lab is open all the time and is centrally located in the middle of campus. It is uncommon to have to wait for a computer, and computer science students are employed in the lab to ensure that the computers work properly. Except for losing information due to file corruption because of the high use of the computers, students have no complaints about computers or the network.

The College Prowler® Grade on

Computers: A

A high grade in Computers designates that computer labs are available, the computer network is easily accessible, and the campus' computing technology is up-to-date.

Facilities

The Lowdown On...
Facilities

Student Center:
Levering Student Union
Mattin Center

Athletic Center:
Ralph S. O'Conner
Recreation Center

Libraries:
2

Campus Size:
140 acres

Popular Places to Chill:
The Beach
Café Q
Freshman Quad
Mattin Center

What Is There to Do on Campus?

Students can work out at the Recreation Center or track, grab a bite to eat at Levering, Megabytes, or Silk Road, attend a play or concert performed by other students, or hang out on the "beach."

Movie Theater on Campus?

No, but several times a month the Film Society uses Shriver Hall to either preview movies before they come out in theaters, or as second release before they come out on video.

Bar on Campus?

No

Bowling on Campus?

No

Coffeehouse on Campus?

Not exactly. There are lots of carts and small shops on campus with seating nearby that sell coffee, like Café Q and Jazzman Café, but there is no distinctive coffeehouse.

Favorite Things to Do

There are several theater groups, many a cappella groups, an improv comedy group, several bands, and a symphony. Because there are so many student arts groups, there are performances almost every weekend. The Recreation Center's basketball courts and climbing wall are popular places for students to meet. E-Level provides free televisions, video games, and pool tables. When the weather is warm enough, students gather in the quads and on "the beach" enjoying the sun. Many students, however, choose to spend time in the library instead of hanging out at other places on campus.

Students Speak Out On...
Facilities

"The athletic center is new and nice. It could use a bit more space, but overall, it's practical. The Mattin Center is a fabulous place to practice instruments. With the new union, people actually go to Levering to hang out."

"**The new athletic center is awesome**, and it's a big student hangout because the student union is basically nonexistent. We have one very nice black box theater for student use, but student groups have to compete for its use. The renovated E-Level is a good place to play pool or video games for free, but most students don't go there now."

"Overall, **the campus is beautiful**, but there's still lots of construction. They built a new recreation center and theater and music rooms recently. The recent senior class gift went into making Levering a real student union; they put in a coffeehouse, restaurants, and made places, in addition to E-Level, for students to hang out."

"The library is really nice, with lots of space to study, but it's underground, which is weird. It's open until 2 a.m. during the semester and 24/7 during finals period. It also has Café Q, which is a good place to get coffee and hang out. There's a fountain-type thing at the Mattin Center, and students hang out there when it's nice. **The Digital Media Center is great**."

"The **varsity facilities aren't very new or modern**, but they get the job done. The school recently improved Levering Hall to make it a student union."

Q "The athletic center was renovated, and an addition was put on. It has several basketball courts, squash courts, a weight room, a cardio room, a rock-climbing wall, a pool, and a room for classes like yoga, kickboxing, and aerobics. There are also additional basketball courts in the older portion of the AC that are used by the varsity teams. **There are two tracks, an indoor 1/10 track, and an outdoor 1/4 track**."

Q "Some facilities on campus have improved, while others need improvements. I am pleased with the Mattin Center and the new student athletic center. I think it's great that Levering hall can finally be claimed as the student union. I, for one, feel that **the cafeteria there is geared more towards the faculty** than towards the students."

Q "There has been massive construction on campus over the past year or so, which should be finished soon. It is mainly for pathways, landscaping, and new buildings for classrooms. **The campus does look really pretty**."

Q "The new student arts center, the Mattin Center, opened up recently. There are quite a few things that go on there by different performing groups. It has **soundproof music rooms**, (some with pianos), and has a black box theater, an Internet café, and darkrooms."

The College Prowler Take On...
Facilities

Hopkins has renovated and is continuing to renovate many facilities on campus due to students' complaints. The campus itself is beautiful. Several years ago, an anonymous donor gave money to replace all asphalt pathways with brick. The quads are landscaped well and surrounded by flowers and trees. E-Level, with its free televisions, video games, and pool tables is popular, but many students still wish it was an on-campus bar. The Mattin Center, Leavering Student Union, and Recreation Center were all built/remodeled in the past few years, and students are happy with these facilities. The main complaint is that although these buildings contain more space for student recreation, music practice, and theater, they are still crowded. On the other hand, these three buildings are state-of-the-art compared to other facilities.

Students have responded well to the renovations that the administration has made. There are plenty of places for student groups to meet, and the campus is well maintained. The Recreation Center and the Mattin Center are grade-A buildings, only losing points because they are not big enough for the interest they have generated. Levering Hall has E-Level, a cafeteria, and large meeting rooms for students fashion shows, dances, and lectures. It didn't, however, have the feel of a real student union in the past, but recent renovations to Levering have proved successful at improving that issue.

B+

The College Prowler® Grade on

Facilities: B+

A high Facilities grade indicates that the campus is aesthetically pleasing and well-maintained; facilities are state-of-the-art, and libraries are exceptional. Other determining factors include the quality of both athletic and student centers and an abundance of things to do on campus.

Campus Dining

The Lowdown On...
Campus Dining

Freshman Meal Plan Requirement?

Yes

Meal Plan Average Cost:

$3,500–$3,900

Places to Grab a Bite with Your Meal Plan:

The Depot
Food: Prepared foods, juice, soda, snacks
Location: Wolman Hall
Hours: Daily 7 a.m.–12 a.m.

Jazzman's Café
Food: Coffee, pastries
Location: Levering lobby
Hours: Monday–Friday
7:30 a.m.–4 p.m.

Levering Food Court

Food: Selection of fast-casual restaurants—Mexican, subs, Italian, burgers, café

Location: Levering Hall

Hours: Sky Ranch Grill, Pete's Arena, and Sub Connections Monday–Friday
10:30 a.m.–2:30 p.m.,
Salsa Rico Monday–Friday
10:30 a.m.–8 p.m.,
Jazzman's Café Monday–Friday
7:30 a.m.–4 p.m.

Megabytes

Food: Grille, Italian, prepared foods, juice, soda, snacks

Location: AMR II residence hall

Hours: Monday–Friday
10 a.m.–10 p.m.,
Saturday 12 p.m.–10 p.m.,
Sunday 2 p.m.–10 a.m.

Terrace Court Café

Food: All-you-can-eat buffet

Location: AMR II residence hall

Hours: Monday–Friday
7 a.m.–8 p.m., Saturday–
Sunday 10 a.m.–8 p.m.

Wolman Station

Food: All-you-can-eat buffet

Location: Wolman Hall

Hours: Monday–Friday
11 a.m.–1:30 p.m., 5 p.m.–
7 p.m., Sunday 10 a.m.–
2 p.m., 5 p.m.–7 p.m.

Off-Campus Places to Use Your Meal Plan:

None, but you can, however, use J-Cash (works like a debit card) from your J-Card at several eateries on and off campus.

24-Hour On-Campus Eating?

No

Student Favorites:

Megabytes

Did You Know?

Café Q has coffee carts located in various buildings on campus. **Café Q is not included in the meal plan**. Silk Road, another eatery not included in the meal plan, is also popular with students. It offers salads, sandwiches, and Chinese cuisine. Megabygtes and Silk Road both offer Internet access to students, as well.

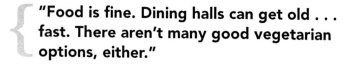

Students Speak Out On...
Campus Dining

> **"Food is fine. Dining halls can get old . . . fast. There aren't many good vegetarian options, either."**

Q "Whenever upperclassmen go back to the dining halls, they always talk about how much better the food has gotten. Although the dining halls don't have the highest quality food, it's not bad, and you have lots of choices about what to eat. Also, **breakfast is the best meal if you're awake for it**."

Q "I've generally found the cafeteria food to be tolerable, if not stellar. **The meal plan has some oddities, though**. Levering cafeteria, which is somewhat included in the meal plan, tends to have the best food and the best social atmosphere."

Q "The food isn't awful in the dining halls, but it isn't spectacular, either. **The best food on campus is probably in Megabytes or Levering**, but you only get credit for half the money you pay for your meal plan, so it's really a rip-off."

Q "The two dining halls are alright. You can 'meal-equiv' at Megabytes or the Depot. **Megabytes is like a grill, and they have pizza, pasta, and calzones**. The Depot really only has breakfast foods like bagels, donuts, and cereal. Wolman and McCoy also have kitchenettes in the suites to make stuff yourself."

Q "**It isn't mom's home-cooking**, but will suffice for four years."

Q "The dining halls really aren't that bad. I am not too picky of an eater, but they always have a lot of choices—salad bar, fresh sandwiches, pizza, burgers, fruit, and desserts. The great thing is that they listen to our suggestions and have improved a lot from my freshmen year. The main freshman dining hall is called Terrace Court, and the sophomore and freshman dining hall is Wolman. There is also Levering, which is not included on the meal plan, but is a little better. That's where the faculty and upperclassmen eat. If you miss your meal in the dining hall or want to eat in your room, **you can 'equiv' your meal for food in either Wolman Depot or Megabytes**."

Q "**The food at Hopkins is like most college food**; it's not bad, but it's not wonderful, either. Megabytes has a fun computer system that you order through for hot sandwiches, fries, quesadillas, and chicken fingers. It also has hot pasta, pizza, and salads. Overall, it's not too bad, but you have to mix it up. The best part about dining is seeing everyone! I spend almost an hour at every meal just talking with everyone. Just be aware of how much you are eating, or you'll gain that Freshman 15."

Q "The meal plans are good. **You choose whether you want a 10, 14, or 19 meals a week**. I had 14 both freshman and sophomore years, and I thought that was good, but I also did not get up for breakfast."

Q "The food on campus is definitely 'ehh.' **There are also lots of great places around campus where you can use J-Cash to buy meals**. This means you get 50 dollars included in your meal plan each semester, and you can use that money at a nearby Middle Eastern place, a couple cafés, grocery stores, Ruby Tuesday, and Orient Express, a sushi place. Check out *www.jcardonline.com* for the listing of vendors. If you miss a meal, you can use your meal points to get food at Megabytes. So, you have a lot of different options for eating."

Q "Food—it sucks. **Really, really sucks**. But, hey, at least you won't get that 'Frosh 15' that all your friends will."

Q "Food is pretty good. There's always pizza and hamburgers, or you can go to Megabytes and 'meal-equiv.' That pretty much means you order what you want, and if it's over $4.50, you have to pay the difference. All I have to say is I am a picky eater, and I gained 20 pounds in five months."

Q "The food on campus leaves a little to be desired. All in all, **food is not a strong suit of JHU**."

Q "The food under the meal plan is okay. It's pretty repetitive and not very healthy. **Almost everything is soaked in grease**. It tastes okay, but will make you fat if you don't watch out."

Q "I got sick of the food on campus after two years. Food doesn't start out too bad, because it's really not. But a few months into school, you'll start to see a pattern, and you'll get tired of it. **It's bearable, and they always have cereal**."

Q "If I had to pick **the worst part about school**, it might be the food."

Q "Personally, I love the food because I'm a junk food addict. **We also have the healthy food** for those other people. I think Megabytes is the best spot on campus. It has couches and a TV, with a table hooked up to computers."

The College Prowler Take On...
Campus Dining

On-campus dining isn't great, but it's edible. What they lose in quality, they make up for in quantity. There are two all-you-can-eat dining halls located near the dorms, which always offer pizza, cereal, salads, burgers, soup, pasta, desserts, and a mix of meats and vegetables. Terrace Court has vegan and Kosher selections, although you have to pay extra for the Kosher meal plan. (*The Dailyjolt* Web site has a menu section, so you can decide where you want to eat based on the food being offered that day.) It is difficult to eat healthily because many of the foods that could be healthy are fried or cooked in butter. You can also meal equiv (buy food á la carte) from Megabytes and the Depot. The Depot has prepared foods like yogurt and chips and bagels, while Megabytes has a grill where you can order fried food, burgers, or Italian. When you figure out the price of the meal plan per meal, however, "meal equiving" (trading in a meal on the meal plan for á la carte items) only gives back half of what you pay. The administration put all new restaurants into Levering as they renovated it. It includes the Jazzman Café, Salsa Rico, Sky Ranch Grill, Pete's Arena, and Sub Connections.

One of the reasons that students complain about the meal plan is that they are required to purchase a meal plan as long as they are living in on-campus housing. The meal plan is expensive. The dining halls get repetitive after several months of eating in them two or three times daily. They offer such a range of foods, though, that you would have to be an incredibly picky eater to fail to find anything.

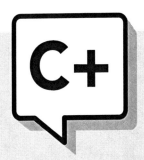

The College Prowler® Grade on

Campus Dining: C+

Our grade on Campus Dining addresses the quality of both school-owned dining halls and independent on-campus restaurants as well as the price, availability, and variety of food.

Off-Campus Dining

The Lowdown On...
Off-Campus Dining

Restaurant Prowler:
Popular Places to Eat!

Akbar Restaurant
Food: Indian
823 N Charles St.
(410) 539-0944
Cool Features: Great lunch buffet at a good price.
Price: $7–$18 per person
Hours: Daily 11:30 a.m.–2:30 p.m., 5 p.m.–11 p.m.

Amicci's
Food: Italian
231 S High St.
(410) 528-1096
Cool Features: Great casual Italian eatery, but the lines can get a bit long, so go early.
Price: $8–$15 per person
Hours: Sunday–Thursday 11:30 a.m.–10 p.m., Friday–Saturday 11:30 a.m.–11 p.m.

Angelo's
Food: Pizza, subs
3600 Keswick Rd.
(410) 235-2595

→

(Angelo's, continued)

Cool Features: They have good, cheap subs, but they're really known for their truly giant slices of pizza. One of these could feed a person for an entire day.

Price: $5–$8 per person

Hours: Monday–Thursday 11 a.m.–10 p.m., Friday–Saturday 11 a.m.–11 p.m., Sunday 12 p.m.–9 p.m.

Bangkok Palace

Food: Thai

5230 York Rd.

(410) 433-0040

Cool Features: The building does not look as though it's a restaurant, but the food is good, and they're helpful if you're not sure what to order.

Price: $9–$12 per person

Hours: Wednesday–Sunday 4 p.m.–10 p.m.

Café Hon

Food: American diner food

1002 W 36th St.

(410) 243-1230

Cool Features: Authentic working-class Baltimore atmosphere.

Price: $5–$12 per person

Hours: Monday–Thursday 7 a.m.–9 p.m., Friday–Saturday 9 a.m.–10 p.m., Sunday 9 a.m.–8 p.m.

Charles Village Pub

Food: American

3107 St. Paul St.

(410) 243-1611

Cool Features: College bar atmosphere; happy hour specials.

Price: $4–$10 per person

Hours: Daily 11:30 a.m.–2 a.m.

The Cheesecake Factory

Food: American, desserts

201 E Pratt St.

(410) 234-3990

Cool Features: Dozens of different cheesecake types to choose from.

Price: $10–$20 per person

Hours: Monday–Thursday 11:30 a.m.–11 p.m., Friday–Saturday 11:30 a.m.–12:30 a.m., Sunday 10 a.m.–10 p.m.

Donna's

Food: Healthy Mediterranean, coffee

800 N Charles St.

(410) 385-0180

Cool Features: Donna herself holds small classes, so you can not only eat her food, but also learn to make it.

Price: $8–$20 per person

Hours: Monday–Thursday 7:30 a.m.–11 p.m., Friday 7:30 a.m.–12 a.m., Saturday 9 a.m.–12 a.m., Sunday 9 a.m.–10 p.m.

ESPN Zone

Food: American

601 E Pratt St.

(410) 685-3776

Cool Features: Great place to go play interactive sports games or watch sports on television.

Price: $10–$15 per person

Hours: Daily 11:30 a.m.– 12 a.m.

Golden West Café

Food: Breakfast, American, vegetarian

842 W 36th St.

(410) 889-8891

Cool Features: This restaurant is in a renovated row house and has a great, down-to-earth atmosphere.

Price: $5–$12 per person

Hours: Monday–Thursday 8 a.m.–10 p.m., Friday–Sunday 8 a.m.–2:30 p.m., 5 p.m.– 10 p.m.

Holy Frijoles

Food: Mexican

908 W 36th St.

(410) 235-2326

Cool Features: Hole in the wall restaurant in Hampden with good food.

Price: $5–$10 per person

Hours: Monday–Friday 11a.m.–1 a.m., Saturday 12 p.m.–1 a.m., Sunday 12 p.m.–10 p.m.

Melting Pot

Food: Fondue

418 York Rd.

(410) 821-6358

Cool Features: The meals take a while, but there isn't a lot of down time. You get multiple courses, and everything is prepared at your table. For the main course, you cook the meat or vegetables in a seasoned sauce yourself.

Price: $30–$50 per person

Hours: Monday–Thursday 5 p.m.–10 p.m., Friday 5 p.m.–11 p.m., Saturday 4 p.m.–11 p.m. Sunday 4 p.m.–9 p.m.

Niwana

Food: Japanese, sushi

3 E 33 St.

(410) 366-4115

Cool Features: Good place to go to escape the dining hall food, and a short walk from campus.

Price: $8–$12 per person

Hours: Monday–Saturday 11:30 a.m.–10:30 p.m., Sunday 3 p.m.–9:30 p.m.

One World Café

Food: American, mostly vegetarian

100 W University Pkwy.

(410) 235-5777

Cool Features: Some unusual and creative dishes, many coffee and drink selections.

Price: $5–$12 per person

(One World Café, continued)

Hours: Monday–Saturday
7:30 a.m.–2 a.m.,
Sunday 8 a.m.–10 p.m.

Paper Moon Diner

Food: American diner,
vegetarian

227 W 29th St.

(410) 889-4444

Cool Features: Interesting
atmosphere with multicolored
walls and unusual decorations
including a large collection of
dolls and Pez dispensers.

Price: $5–$14 per person

Hours: Daily 24 hours

Paul Chen's Hong Kong Restaurant

Food: Chinese

2426 N Charles St.

(410) 235-8744

Cool Features: Good Chinese
food and a great menu of fake
meat dishes.

Price: $7–$15 per person

Hours: Daily 11 a.m.–11 p.m.

Pete's Grille

Food: Breakfast

3130 Greenmount Ave.

(410) 467-7698

Cool Features: Great place
to grab a good old fashioned
breakfast. The lines can get
pretty long, so you might want
to wake up early. The good
news is that it's within walking
distance of Hopkins.

(Pete's Grille, continued)

Price: $5–$7 per person

Hours: Monday–Saturday
7 a.m.–1:30 a.m.,
Sunday 8 a.m.–1 a.m.

Rocky Run Tap & Grill

Food: American, kid's menu

3105 St. Paul St.

(410) 235-2501

Cool Features: They serve
their own Canadian-style
microbrews and great desserts

Price: $8–$25 per person

Hours: Monday–Thursday
11 a.m.–1 a.m., Friday–
Saturday 11 a.m.–2 a.m.,
Sunday 11 a.m.–12 a.m.

Ruby Tuesday

Food: American

3003 N Charles St.

(410) 467-8155

Cool Features: Ruby Tuesday
has the consistency of good
chain food, meaning you're
guaranteed to be able to
find food just like at the one
at home.

Price: $10–$15 per person

Hours: Monday–Thursday
11 a.m.–11 p.m., Friday–
Saturday 11 a.m.–12 a.m.,
Sunday 11 a.m.–10 p.m.

Silk Road

Food: Pan-Asian

Mattin Center, JHU campus

(410) 516-0426

Cool Features: Winner, of Baltimore City Paper's "Best Cheap Restaurant" award.

Price: $7–&12 per person

Hours: Monday–Friday 11 a.m.–6 p.m.

Tamber's Nifty Fifties Diner

Food: American diner and Indian

3327 St. Paul St.

Cool Features: Indian food in a fifties diner.

Price: $6–$12 per person

Thai Landing

Food: Thai

3316 Greenmount Ave.

(410) 727-1234

Cool Features: Good Thai food near campus

Price: $6–$14 per person

Hours: Monday–Thursday 11:30 a.m.–2:40 p.m., 5 p.m.–9:30 p.m., Friday–Saturday 5 p.m.–10:10 p.m.

Vaccaro's

Food: Dessert

222 Albemarle St.

(410) 685-4905

Cool Features: The best place to get a great Italian dessert. It's all they do, and they do it very well.

Price: $5–$8 per person

Hours: Monday 9 a.m.– 10 p.m., Tuesday–Sunday 9 a.m.–11 p.m.

Xando

Food: Coffeeshop, American

3003 N Charles St.

(410) 889-7076

Cool Features: Great place for coffee and s'mores; sometimes they have poetry readings.

Price: $5–$9 per person

Hours: Monday–Thursday 7 a.m.–11 p.m., Friday 6 a.m.–12 a.m., Saturday 8 a.m.–12 a.m., Sunday 8 a.m.–11 p.m.

Closest Grocery Stores:

Eddie's Market
3117 St. Paul St.
Baltimore, MD 21218
(410) 889-1558

Giant at the Rotunda
711 W. 40th St.
Baltimore, MD 21211
(410) 467-0417

Safeway
2401 N Charles St.
Baltimore, MD 21218
(410) 261-6110

Superfresh Food Market
1020 W 41st St.
Baltimore, MD 21211
(410) 243-0001

Student Favorites:

Akbar Restaurant
Charles Village Pub
Niwana
One World Café
Rocky Run Tap & Grill

Student Specials:

None, however, Ruby Tuesday has a "buy one drink, get the second for a penny" deal.

24-Hour Eating:

Paper Moon Diner

Best Pizza:

Angelo's

Best Chinese:

Paul Chen's Chinese Restaurant

Best Breakfast:

Pete's Grille

Best Wings:

Charles Village Pub

Best Healthy:

One World Café

Best Place to Take Your Parents:

Any restaurant at the Inner Harbor

Other Places to Check Out:

Hard Rock Café
India Tandoor
McDonald's
Orient Express
Papa Salis

Did You Know?

Baltimore is known for its local blue crabs, and **crab dishes are abundant**, especially steamed crabs and crab cakes.

Every fall, one of the stadiums hosts a **chocolate festival** that raises money for charity.

Maryland's **second largest Farmers' Market** takes place every Saturday morning throughout the year just four blocks from Hopkins.

Students Speak Out On...
Off-Campus Dining

{ **"Baltimore is full of all types of restaurants that I can guarantee will satisfy your pallet."**

Q "**There are a whole lot of restaurants right around Hopkins that serve good food** no matter what you like, and almost all are within a college student's budget. There's Chinese, Thai, vegan, pizza as cheap as four dollars for a large, and my personal favorite, Indian. In fact Tamber's Nifty Fifties doubles as a vintage 1950s-era diner, with burgers, shakes, and a jukebox. Try a milkshake with a spicy Indian dish; it's surprisingly good."

Q "Hopkins has one of the most unique restaurants in the country. Prices at the Paper Moon Diner may be kind of steep (between six and twelve dollars an entrée), but the food is good. **The atmosphere is bizarre**, with mannequin parts adorning the walls, fake ivy crawling the ceiling, and a toilet on the front lawn. It's open 24 hours, and students love late-night study breaks there."

Q "No matter what kind of food you like, you'll find great restaurants in Baltimore! **It's a big enough city to have at least one restaurant of almost every ethnic variety**. There are some restaurants you can walk to, but others are worth driving or taking a cab. In my opinion, Paul Chen's for Chinese, India Tandoor for cheap India buffet (about $5 for all-you-can-eat), Holy Frijoles for Mexican, Amicci' for Italian, Thai Landing for Thai, Papa Salis for pizza, and Angelo's for subs."

Q "There **aren't many restaurants within walking distance**. My favorite restaurant is vegan-friendly One World Café."

Q "There is another advantage to all the colleges nearby—Baltimore has **lots of good cheap restaurants**. Right near Hopkins Rocky Run, Niwana, and Orient Express are all good options, though very different from one another. Farther away (but still within walking distance), Holy Frijoles is tasty, cheap, and has big portions. Little Italy has a range of restaurants from cozy eateries to high-end dining."

Q "Off campus, **there are plenty of restaurant on St. Paul**. There is Rocky Run, my personal favorite, which has typical burgers and sandwiches Cajun-style. There's also Donna's, which has coffee and pretty unique food. Niwana has Japanese, Korean, and sushi. One World Café on the other side of campus serves vegetarian and other healthy food. There is a Ruby Tuesday on North Charles."

Q "There are about 10 restaurants within walking distance from the campus, including coffee places in which you can also eat. **We also have a great coffee stand with treats in the library**, at Gilman, Bloomberg, and the Mattin Center. These are great for late-night study sessions, or a morning kick of caffeine."

Q "**My favorite restaurants are Xando's, Donna's, and Niwana**. If you drive or take a cab, there are a ton of restaurants near the mall, in the Harbor, and in Little Italy, which are all only 10 minutes away. Honestly, I only eat out about once a month because of time and money. I do love to go out to coffee and talk, though, and there are great places for that nearby."

Q "**Off-campus food is amazing**. My personal favorites are Tamber's Nifty Fifty's, which has traditional American food as well as Indian cuisine, and Silk Road which has great Chinese food. Both are relatively cheap."

Q "I don't go out to eat much, but there's a really good Little Italy here. **The Chinese food out here leaves much to be desired, though**. There aren't any fast food places nearby, either. There's a McDonald's about 15 minutes away, but you have to walk through the ghetto, and they don't usually have sauce for their nuggets."

Q "There are a lot of great places to go in the Inner Harbor of Baltimore, but often, people eat on campus or order in. **Living in college puts you on a budget**, so we didn't eat out a whole lot freshman year."

The College Prowler Take On...
Off-Campus Dining

There are a variety of restaurants around Baltimore, enough to satisfy even the pickiest eaters. Only about 15 of these restaurants are within walking distance of Hopkins, though. The Hopkins and Colltown shuttles, or access to a car, will greatly increase your culinary options. Students mainly cite the lack of time and money as reasons they don't get out to eat more, not the restaurant selection. Because Hopkins has such a diverse student body, you will likely find that students go to ethnic restaurants at least as frequently as ones that serve American cuisine. Students suggest a variety of restaurants including Xando, Ruby Tuesday, Rocky Run, Niwana, Holy Frijoles, and Thai Landing.

While at Hopkins, make sure you get out at least occasionally to sample the restaurants Baltimore has to offer. Because Baltimore has many college students and young professionals, there are numerous places where you can get a meal for under 10 dollars. There are even places where you can get a meal for five or six dollars, and still bring home leftovers. Students need to make the effort to try restaurants around Baltimore, in addition to ones adjacent to Hopkins, and they'll be sure to find a new favorite.

The College Prowler® Grade on
Off-Campus Dining: A

A high Off-Campus Dining grade implies that off-campus restaurants are affordable, accessible, and worth visiting. Other factors include the variety of cuisine and the availability of alternative options (vegetarian, vegan, Kosher, etc.).

Campus Housing

The Lowdown On...
Campus Housing

Room Types:
Single, double, and triple rooms, suites, and apartments

Undergrads Living on Campus:
61%

Best Dorms:
AMR I and II

Worst Dorms:
Buildings A and B

Number of Dormitories:
6

Number of University-Owned Apartments:
3

Dormitories:

AMR I and II
Floors: 3
Total Occupancy: 510
Bathrooms: Communal
Coed: Yes
Residents: Freshmen
Room Types: Single, doubles
Special Features: Cable ready, Ethernet hookup, computer lab, study hall, multi-purpose room, laundry facilities, and houses Megabytes, the Housing Office, Residential Office, exercise room, Student Health and Wellness

Bradford Hall
Floors: 9
Total Occupancy: 151
Bathrooms: In apartment
Coed: By apartment
Residents: Upperclassmen
Room Types: Singles in one-, two-, and three-bedroom apartments
Special Features: Cable ready, Ethernet hookup, laundry facilities, exercise room, air-conditioning

Buildings A and B
Floors: 3
Total Occupancy: 195
Bathrooms: In suite
Coed: By suite
Residents: Freshmen, upperclassmen
Room Types: Singles and doubles; four people to a suite
Special Features: Cable ready, Ethernet hookup, social lounge, laundry facilities, air-conditioning

Homewood Apartments
Floors: 6
Total Occupancy: 220
Bathrooms: In apartment
Coed: By apartment
Residents: Upperclassmen
Room Types: Singles in one-, two-, three-, and four-bedrooms
Special Features: Cable ready, Ethernet hookup, laundry facilities, exercise room, air-conditioning, 24-hour security guard

Ivy Hall

Floors: 4

Total Occupancy: 48

Bathrooms: In apartment

Coed: By apartment

Residents: Upperclassmen

Room Types: Single in four-bedroom apartments

Special Features: Cable ready, Ethernet hookup, laundry facilities, air-conditioning, furnished apartments

McCoy Hall

Floors: 7

Total Occupancy: 510

Bathrooms: In suite

Coed: By suite

Residents: Freshmen, upperclassmen

Room Types: Singles and doubles; four people to a suite

Special Features: Cable ready, Ethernet hookup, study hall, multipurpose room, Housing Office, social lounge with cable television in each hall, air-conditioning, 24-hour security guard

Wolman Hall

Floors: 7

Total Occupancy: 474

Bathrooms: In suite

Coed: By suite

Residents: Freshmen, upperclassmen

Room Types: Singles and doubles; four people to a suite

Special Features: Cable ready, Ethernet hookup, exercise room, Wolman Station Dining Hall, the Depot, lounges, laundry facilities, air-conditioning, 24-hour security guard

Bed Type

Twin extra-long

Cleaning Service?

Yes, every day during the week, there is a cleaning service for all public areas. Hallways, social areas, and communal bathrooms are cleaned.

Available for Rent

In the AMRs and Buildings A and B, students are forbidden from bringing their own refrigerator or microwave, but they can rent either a refrigerator or a refrigerator with microwave.

You Get

Bed, desk, chair, three drawers, wardrobe, Internet and cable (for a cost)

Also Available

Substance-free housing, single-sex housing

Did You Know?

Undergraduates are **required to live on campus freshman and sophomore years**, unless they live with their parents.

Residential Assistants (RAs) plan **at least three social activities a month** to encourage students to interact with each other and enjoy themselves.

If any damage occurs in the common area of a dorm, the Housing Department **immediately bills all students** who live in that particular hall.

Students Speak Out On...
Campus Housing

"AMRs were fun, but it's an experience I would never want to relive. Lack of air-conditioning and having to live with a roommate weren't fun. Dorms will never be that fabulous, but they're decent."

Q "The AMRs are great for hanging out and getting to know people in your hall. Most people who live in the AMRs love it. **Wolman is pretty good if you want air-conditioning and your own bathroom**. It doesn't have a social atmosphere like the AMRs, but still has a good mix of freshman and sophomores, so it's friendly. Buildings A, B, and McCoy aren't that great because they have settings that don't facilitate sociality."

Q "**Live in the AMRs freshman year** if you want an experience similar to that described in movies. It's really chill and so easy to meet people. You probably won't get a single, so try to find something in common with your roommate. Also, no matter where you live, bring decorations! The rooms are really bare and unattractive, otherwise."

Q "What dorms are best depends on what you like. The **AMRs are an intense, social, freshman experience**. Wolman and McCoy have more privacy and amenities, but they can be a little isolating. Buildings A and B have the worst of both, and they're the most likely to be tripled when the dorms are overcrowded early in the year."

Q "AMR II is especially bad. **Ask for Wolman or McCoy first if you can**, unless you don't mind being surrounded by freshmen."

Q "The dorms vary greatly in quality. The AMRs are the typical freshman dorms. They're not nice, but they're very social. **Buildings A and B are suite-style, and they're fairly nice**. You share a bathroom with four people. Wolman and McCoy are suites, too, but they are nicer and have kitchenettes in each suite. They are less social, though, and house some sophomores. If you want a single room, you'll have to live in the AMRs or in Buildings A and B."

Q "The dorms are typical of any college. I lived in the AMRs freshman year, which are the most social, although not as nice. They are typical double rooms on a hallway, with bathrooms down the halls. All dorms, except a few, are coed. The downfall of the AMRs is that there is no air-conditioning; however, fans in the fall and spring are more than sufficient. **I would not have given up my AMR experience for anything**, and would not have lived anywhere else. I met all of the friends that I have now in those dorms and had a great freshman year."

Q "**AMRs are much more social**—better for your freshman year."

Q "In Wolman and McCoy, where I lived this year, the rooms are suite-style, which means four people share a bathroom and have a kitchen. It's a lot nicer; **the rooms are air conditioned and carpeted**."

Q "**Stay in the AMRs the first year**. You'll meet so many more people that way. There's McCoy and Wolman, which are like suites. You really don't meet many people. It's kind of like living in a hotel."

Q "I was in the AMR, and I liked it very much. We were all really close in the building. **It was very friendly**, and we had fun together."

Q "The dorms are nice. My room as a freshman was huge. **If you want big rooms, live in Buildings A or B**. Their only downfalls are central heat and air, and they have mice. They also aren't very social, so if you are shy, go elsewhere. The AMRs are the most social and most freshmen live there. They have no AC, mice, and very small rooms. Wolman Hall has AC and heat in each of the rooms, and it has no mice. The rooms given to freshmen in Wolman tend to be tiny."

Q "**Avoid Wolman and McCoy as a freshman**. You really won't meet people on your floor there. My floor was a big part of my life freshman year, and people in Wolman and McCoy are usually sophomores who already have friends. Buildings A and B are set up suite-style, which some might say makes it harder to meet people. But since they're freshman dorms, people don't know each other. You'll still meet everyone on your floor."

Q "The dorms aren't that bad. As a freshman, you will most likely be living in the AMRs, Buildings A or B, or Wolman Hall. The AMRs are like regular dorms. All are coed except for a wing in AMR I, which is all female, and one in AMR II, which is all male. They have communal bathrooms and smaller rooms. **They are the most social places to live, and are generally the best for freshman** that want to get to know people. Buildings A and B are suite-style dorms. It is more fun to have a place in Wolman or McCoy sophomore year with three of your friends."

The College Prowler Take On...
Campus Housing

On-campus housing is required for freshmen and sophomores. AMR I and II offer the quintessential dorm experience. Almost all rooms are yellow-walled, two-person squares. These are the most popular dorms because of the "freshman" feel to them. The dorms are very social and people form close friendships. Freshmen often call it incest when you hook up with someone in your hall since you're going to run into them at breakfast, dinner, and on the way to the bathroom for the rest of the year. Buildings A and B are what most freshmen think that they want. They claim to have that same freshman feel except with air-conditioning and toilets in their suites. But each of these buildings is tiny compared with the AMRs, which each have hundreds of students. Many of these students feel isolated from the bustle of the AMRs. For students who want a quieter freshman living experience, Buildings A and B and Wolman and McCoy are great options. Wolman and McCoy dorms are located about five minutes from the freshman dorms, but the mix of freshmen and sophomores gives them a more mature feel. The arrangement is suites with a common room on each floor.

On-campus housing isn't spectacular, but it is acceptable. Since Hopkins has a small campus, all of the dorms that are exclusively freshmen are located near each other. The dorms that contain older students also are located nearby. Common areas are cleaned frequently, but on the weekends, they dirty quickly. On-campus housing is expensive, and it requires the purchase of a meal plan. All on- campus housing is monitored by Hop Cops or security personnel, and is located near classrooms, dining halls, and other campus buildings.

B

The College Prowler® Grade on
Campus Housing: B

A high Campus Housing grade indicates that dorms are clean, well-maintained, and spacious. Other determining factors include variety of dorms, proximity to classes, and social atmosphere.

Off-Campus Housing

The Lowdown On...
Off-Campus Housing

Undergrads in Off-Campus Housing:
39%

Average Rent For:
1BR Apt: $600–$700/month
2BR Apt: $800–$900/month
3BR Apt: $1,000–$1,100/month

Popular Areas:
Charles Village
University Parkway

For Assistance Contact:
www.jhu.edu/~hds/offcampus
offcampus@hd.jhu.edu

Best Time to Look for a Place:
Figure out who you want to live with by Intersession sophomore year, and start looking at the beginning of second semester.

Students Speak Out On...
Off-Campus Housing

"Hopkins requires students to live on campus for the first two years, and provides little to no housing for juniors or seniors, so there really isn't any other choice for students."

Q "**The apartments and row-houses right around Hopkins are cost-effective** if you know where to look. In fact, you'll probably spend less money living off campus than you did in the dorms. The option is there, though, for those who want to spend more and have nicer housing. Think about who you want to live with, because you won't be right down the hall from your other friends anymore."

Q "Depending on whether you want a house or an apartment, **it can be very easy to find housing**. If you want to live right next to campus or in a particular apartment building, contact a landlord or get on a waiting list early. If you're open to living several blocks from campus, you'll easily find something. Housing is a lot cheaper in Baltimore than in many other cities, but you want to make sure that you are careful walking to and from campus."

Q "Off-campus housing is so much better. **It's great not to have to have a roommate** and be on the meal plan."

Q "I have lived in off-campus, University-sponsored housing for the past two years, and I have had a good experience overall, but I have some complaints. I think **JHU did a good job renovating and furnishing the apartments** for students, but I had problems with getting things fixed, among other things."

Q "Everyone lives off campus junior and senior year, unless they're a RA. It's very convenient. There are lots of apartments and row-houses available for students. The row-houses are like townhouses, but they're in a sketchier part of town. **Guys tend to rent them more often than girls**."

Q "**Off-campus housing is very convenient**. It is plentiful and often very cheap. It's not hard to find housing your junior year, although you have to live in University housing the first two years. Still, if you get a good lotto number your sophomore year, you could get a sweet University-owned apartment. My friend has four singles and two baths close to campus."

Q "It's not too hard to find an apartment off campus. **You're only guaranteed to live on campus for your first two years**, so everyone has to find something after that. Some people also opt to live in row-houses, but either way, it's not too bad to find a place to live. You'll probably know some upperclassmen that will pass down their place to you."

Q "Finding off-campus housing is pretty difficult, but it helps to know older students so you can get their house or apartment after they graduate. **Greeks and athletes have an easier time** because they tend to know the older students."

Q "Finding off-campus housing **isn't as hard as I thought** it would be. I was a little frustrated by it because it seems so daunting, but the outskirts of campus are full of apartment buildings and row-houses. Living off campus is actually cheaper than living on campus, and as long as you get your name on a waiting list early, you should be fine."

Q "Housing is fairly easy to find off campus, and **the most you'll walk to any class is 15 to 20 minutes**."

Q "Housing off campus is very convenient. **The college provides apartments** and also suite-like buildings to live in. Your first year you probably won't live in them, but as soon as sophomore year you can live in the apartments. They're really big. Around the campus is a residential area with lots of little restaurants and shops, so there are places for you to live there, too. Most of us would love to stay in college housing. It's so much easier."

The College Prowler Take On...
Off-Campus Housing

Off-campus housing is cheap and convenient. If you are open to living anywhere within four blocks of campus, housing is also plentiful, with students living in one through four bedroom apartments and row-houses. It is more difficult to find housing directly across the street from the University, but not impossible if you look early. Students are spread out in every direction from campus, so no matter where you choose to live, you are likely to find other students as your neighbors. Make sure you go through the building carefully before signing the lease; landlords aren't known for keeping the buildings in good shape. Even though you will not have trouble finding housing, expect to look on your own. It's a good idea to ask upperclassmen to talk with their landlords and put in a good word for you. Many students have not found the off-campus housing office to be helpful.

Finding off-campus housing won't prove to be an issue, but students don't like that Hopkins has almost no upperclassmen housing options after requiring students to live on campus for their first two years. Housing is plentiful, and Baltimore has low property prices. The problem lies in that students often forget that they live in a city, and that they need to be concerned with security. Students have been robbed walking to and from their houses, and many student houses have been burglarized. If you live in a row-house, lock your doors all the time and find a place with bars on your windows. If you keep a few basic safety guidelines in mind, however, you should have a great experience living off campus.

The College Prowler® Grade on

Off-Campus
Housing: B+

A high grade in Off-Campus Housing indicates that apartments are of high quality, close to campus, affordable, and easy to secure.

Diversity

The Lowdown On...
Diversity

Native American:
1%

White:
61%

Asian American:
22%

International:
5%

African American:
6%

Out-of-State:
81%

Hispanic:
6%

Political Activity

Many students complain about the apathetic nature of other students. However, in the past few years, the Middle East and the War in Iraq were subjects of frequent debates and newsletter editorials. Although there is a relatively even split of Republicans and Democrats, students lean more to the conservative than to the liberal side.

Gay Pride

There is a very active group on campus for homosexual, bisexual, and transgendered persons: the Diverse Gender and Sexuality Alliance. This group holds office hours, weekly meetings, club nights, and Awareness Days—which is a month-long series of events that includes lectures by high-profile speakers, movies, and educational discussions.

Most Popular Religions

Hopkins was founded as a research University with specifications that it favor no particular religion. It would be difficult to find a religion not represented at Hopkins, although many students do not practice any religion. There is a very active Interfaith Center, which encourages discussion between religious groups and holds services for many of them.

Minority Clubs

Some minority clubs include the Black Student Union, Caribbean, Chinese, Hellenic, Indian, Korean, Middle Eastern, InterAsian Council, Organizacion Latina Estudiantil (OLE), NAACP, Pakistani, Persian, Russian, Scandinavian, and Spanish groups, as well as the International Club. If you don't feel as though your ethnic group is represented, it is very easy to start a student group.

Students Speak Out On...
Diversity

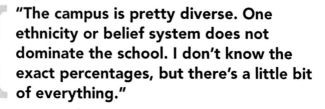

"The campus is pretty diverse. One ethnicity or belief system does not dominate the school. I don't know the exact percentages, but there's a little bit of everything."

Q "It seems to me like **we have students from lots of different countries** and a relatively large amount of open-mindedness. But considering the fact that we live in a city with one of the highest percentages of African Americans, they're not well represented at Hopkins."

Q "A lot of people here complain that we're not diverse enough. There are students here from around the world, but many of them only become friends with people of their nationality. When you look around, **there are lots of different homogenous groups,** and only a few groups with friends of many ethnicities. Some minorities don't like when white students try to learn about their culture."

Q "Hopkins isn't terribly diverse. Hopkins has a large number of international students, but **the domestic contingent tends to be mostly white** with a decent Asian population, as well. The student body also tends strongly towards upper-middle-class backgrounds."

Q "Racially, we're pretty diverse. However, **there are still racial cliques,** which isn't cool."

Q "It is **a very diverse campus for a college**— internationally, racially, and religiously. I'm used to NYC, so nothing is that diverse."

Q "The campus is diverse, though, it can be segregated. There are many culture clubs that promote diversity. I would say **the biggest minorities represented are Indians and Asians**—both foreign-born and American. The least represented are probably the Hispanics and African Americans."

Q "Campus is really diverse. I've met so many different types of people. My freshman year roommate went to a boarding school, my current roommate was from the mountains of New Hampshire, and **there were people on my floor from Korea and Turkey**. I've met lots of cool and friendly people."

Q "Hopkins is the most diverse campus you will ever see. No joke. I went to an extremely diverse high school, yet I was amazed when I came here. **It's so nice to have different friends who can speak so many different languages**, have different views, and cook different foods. You have to mooch off of your ethnic friends here. Don't miss out!"

Q "Diversity is possibly the most defining feature of Hopkins. We have **a very diverse population with people from all over the United States and abroad**. It's one of my favorite aspects, because people are from all different backgrounds and all so unique."

Q "There is **some diversity of skin color**. There is a fairly large Asian population. There are a lot of African Americans in Baltimore, but on campus, it doesn't make up that large of a percentage. There are only a few Hispanics, but a fairly large Jewish population."

The College Prowler Take On...
Diversity

Hopkins students disagree about diversity at Hopkins. A recent survey showed that while many white students thought that Hopkins was very diverse, minority students disagreed. Hopkins does have larger Asian and Indian populations, and smaller African American and Hispanic populations. In addition, there are fewer students from Western Europe, and many more from Eastern Europe. While the University is diverse presently, it is working towards greater diversity. Students also believe that it needs to work on integrating students of different races. As one student said, "The campus is diverse, though, it can be segregated." Some students choose not to learn about other cultures or become friends with people of other cultures while attending Hopkins, but there are many opportunities to develop a diverse groups of friends.

Hopkins has more racial diversity than other colleges in Baltimore, but it represents some minorities more significantly than others. The administration has been unable to break up cliques among people of the same ethnicity, and while some students like the ethnic bond, it makes other students feel excluded. Also, Hopkins is not very diverse economically. Most students are from middle- to upper-middle-class families. This creates a feeling of separation between students and individuals who live in and around Baltimore. Students from many races will find that their ethnicity has organized a student group, and students have ample opportunities to learn about the food, culture, and history of their own or other ethnicities.

The College Prowler® Grade on

Diversity: B+

A high grade in Diversity indicates that ethnic minorities and international students have a notable presence on campus and that students of different economic backgrounds, religious beliefs, and sexual preferences are well-represented.

Guys & Girls

The Lowdown On...
Guys & Girls

Men Undergrads:
53%

Women Undergrads:
47%

Birth Control Available?
Yes, just ask at the Student Health and Wellness Office.

Social Scene

Hopkins is a school with many serious students. There's a lot of interaction between the sexes because nearly all freshmen housing and classes are coed. (If you end up in a few art history, classics, or engineering classes, you might find that your class is almost entirely single-sex.) When students have free time, they are as likely to spend it with members of the opposite sex as with members of their own sex. Students are most social when they're involved with extracurricular activities, and when they are at parties or clubs on the weekends.

Hookups or Relationships?

Hookups are most common freshman year, especially in the AMRs. When students want to hookup with someone they don't know as well, they often go to frat parties. Many students enter Hopkins with boyfriends or girlfriends at other schools, and prefer these relationships because they take up less time. Time is the major barrier that prevents more students from wanting relationships. Relationships do occur, however, usually arising from friendships in dorms, classes, or extracurricular activities.

Best Place to Meet Guys/Girls

Because students are so focused and busy, the best place to meet members of the opposite sex is by scoping them out during daily activities. There are advantages to this. When you meet someone in your dorm, you don't have to go through the charade of calling at the right time and dressing up for dates because both of you are just kind of "there." When you meet someone in a class or an extracurricular activity, you have a common interest that can help you get to know each other better. Other places that Hopkins students meet members of the opposite sex, and which allows them to pursue a more traditional dating relationship, are through friends, at the library, HAC lab, parties, and clubs.

Dress Code

The daily dress code is very casual. Both guys and girls wear jeans and khakis to class and around campus. Guys generally wear T-shirts or button-down shirts, and girls usually wear T-shirts, sweaters, or tank tops. Because many students have professional internships, it is also not uncommon to see sport coats or skirts around campus, especially on Thursdays and Fridays, when many students don't have classes. When going to bars or parties, girls usually dress up more than guys, wearing high heels, skirts or nice pants, and cute shirts.

Did You Know?

Top Places to Find Hotties:

1. Class
2. Recreation Center
3. Frat parties

Top Places to Hook Up:

1. AMRs
2. The 'beach'
3. MSE Library
4. Bloomberg roof by the telescope
5. Back of a security escort van

"It's a college. There are a several thousand people. Just about any type you'd be looking for, you can find. If you can't, there are four other colleges nearby to look at, too."

Q "JHU is known for having unattractive people, but I found they have **a pretty average share of attractive and unattractive people**. The main difference is that most students at JHU don't put as much time into their appearance. What struck me the most coming to Baltimore from the South was the difference in the general attitude of people; students here seem a little more withdrawn."

Q "There's such a range of looks here because there are people from so many countries. Foreign students don't really seem interested in dating. **They're more interested in studying or hanging out** with groups of people of the same sex. Or people have serious relationships. After freshman year, there's not a lot of hooking up."

Q "**There are hot people here**, especially if you're looking for preppy people. They're everywhere. Watch out, though, because it's a big enough school that not everyone knows everyone else, but you'll know someone who knows everyone. Reputations get built quickly."

Q "Guys and girls are decent looking. **'Hot' is a relative term.**"

Q "The **guys get mixed reviews**. I think they're fine, but others disagree."

Q "I think that there are a lot of students at Hopkins that are very driven academically and tend to be less involved in social activities. They sometimes **tend not to care about their appearances** and may appear less attractive physically. They may also need to work on their social skills. However, there are also many students that are academically driven and also make time for social activities, sports, clubs, working out, music, theater, and other activities. I think that the best way to meet people at Hopkins is to get involved in different activities and organizations. By doing this, you'll meet a diverse group of people."

Q "**The campus is mostly devoid of nice-looking people**. Needless to say, moving here from Los Angeles was quite a shock. I would like to consider myself a well-dressed, attractive person, and I have to do most of my shopping in DC or back home in California."

Q "Well, apparently **we're never ranked that high in magazine polls of hotness**, but I don't think we're too bad. I've had several crushes, one serious boyfriend, and a couple flings. I guess we're about average. There are other schools nearby if you don't like the Hopkins pickings."

Q "**The ratio of guys to girls is 50:50**. As with any top school, there are people who choose to study all the time and not go out, and those who go out all the time and barely study. And, of course, there are people in between. It is possible to find your kind of people at Hopkins because there are so many different kinds. I've found that people are pretty down-to-earth and caring. I've made some really great friends. In terms of hotness, it depends on your taste!"

Q "Most students are very, very studious. JHU has never done much to sponsor campus life, and it is **famous for poor social life**."

Q "There are more guys than girls, so the **girls always have an easier time finding someone**. Guys often knock the girls as not hot, but I think it's a fair selection."

Q "The **guys are hot**, especially the lacrosse players, the swimmers, the water polo guys, and the frat guys. I am not boy-obsessed!"

Q "Well, I personally don't think the guys are that hot, but that's just me. My friends think that there are tons of hot guys. It **all depends on your personal preference**. I tend to like preppy guys, and there aren't many of those here. If you like tough, big, broad guys, you're in luck. The girls aren't too hot, either. Most of them are really unattractive, but those that aren't unattractive are gorgeous. There really aren't too many average-looking girls at Hopkins."

Q "There's **such a variety of people** it's kind of hard to generalize. I've met so many types of people from all over. There are complete computer dorks, preppy boarding school kids, and normal, down-to-earth people. My friends and I always joke that all the hot guys are hiding somewhere on campus."

Q "Being a girl here is fun. In high school, guys didn't pay much attention to me, but at Hopkins **frats there are always guys to chill with**."

Q "I must say that **the aesthetically-pleasing pool of men is larger than the women's**. The girls are ugly, and the guys are okay. A few are hot here and there, but not really amazing."

Q "Both sexes complain about the other's lack of 'hotness.' I've seen **a handful of decent girls**, but really not a large number. Most of the girls I'm friends with play for the women's ultimate Frisbee team, so I didn't meet them on the basis of anything but ultimate. I dated three girls—one at Hopkins, all ultimate-related—so I wasn't really looking elsewhere."

The College Prowler Take On...
Guys & Girls

People get accepted into Hopkins because of their intelligence, not because of their attractiveness. That isn't to say that there aren't attractive people at Hopkins. The biggest difference is that students at Hopkins pay less attention to their appearance than students at other schools. There's no one type of person that dominates Hopkins. There are preppy people, jocks, and foreign students. Girls like the near 50:50 ratio of guys to girls, and it isn't hard to meet people of the opposite sex since almost all dorms are coed. In the AMRs, there are a decent number of hookups, but many of them aren't too serious. By sophomore year, there are less hookups and more relationships, which tend to be based on common interests, not looks. Even so, many students go through Hopkins without having a boyfriend or girlfriend. If you are upset by the selections at Johns Hopkins, you can easily travel to several other area colleges to meet more people.

On the whole, Hopkins is a pretty average campus when it comes to looks. There aren't many, if any, models running around. (There's a running joke on campus about the pick-up line for attractive people being "You must go to Towson/Loyola.") The population is diverse, so there's no traditional look here. Most of the students are pretty down-to-earth and studious. Even if you don't end up dating anyone, you will, at the very least, make friends with members of the opposite sex.

The College Prowler® Grade on
Guys: B+

A high grade for Guys indicates that the male population on campus is attractive, smart, friendly, and engaging, and that the school has a decent ratio of guys to girls.

The College Prowler® Grade on
Girls: C+

A high grade for Girls not only implies that the women on campus are attractive, smart, friendly, and engaging, but also that there is a fair ratio of girls to guys.

Athletics

The Lowdown On...
Athletics

Athletic Division:
NCAA Division III,
Division I for water polo
and lacrosse

Conference:
Centennial Conference

School Mascot:
Blue Jay

→

Men's Varsity Sports:

Baseball

Basketball

Crew

Cross-Country

Fencing

Football

Lacrosse

Soccer

Swimming & Diving

Tennis

Track & Field (Indoor and Outdoor)

Water polo

Wrestling

Women's Varsity Sports:

Basketball

Crew

Cross-Country

Fencing

Field Hockey

Lacrosse

Soccer

Swimming & Diving

Tennis

Track & Field (Indoor and Outdoor)

Volleyball

Club Sports:

Cheerleading

Cycling (Men's and Women's)

Golf

Ice Hockey

Lacrosse

Martial Arts

Rugby

Soccer

Table Tennis

Tennis

Ultimate Frisbee

Intramurals:

Badminton

Basketball

Cycling

Flag Football

Floor Hockey

Foosball

Lacrosse

Racquetball

Road Racing

Soccer

Softball

Squash

Swimming

Table Tennis

Tennis

Track & Field

Ultimate Frisbee

Volleyball

Wrestling

Athletic Fields
Homewood Field

Getting Tickets
Call (410) 516-7490. Tickets are easy to get—cheap for the
general public, and free for students.

Most Popular Sports
Lacrosse is by far the most popular sport and is one of few
Division I sports at Hopkins. The Blue Jays are one of the best
teams in the nation every year.

Overlooked Teams
The fencing team is Division I and competitive against much
bigger schools, but gets very little recognition. The baseball
team had an excellent record in the past few years, and
was one of the top Division III teams in the nation, despite
frequently playing home games in front of crowds numbering
in the teens.

Best Place to Take a Walk
Wyman Park winds by a stream behind the school. Roland Park
provides tree-lined streets and leads to Sherwood Gardens.

Gyms/Facilities
Ralph S. O'Conner Recreation Center
The new gym opened in January of 2002. It has squash,
basketball, and racquetball courts, a swimming pool, martial
arts and fitness classrooms, a fitness room, a weight room,
and a climbing wall. In addition, they have equipment for
badminton, table tennis, volleyball, and racquet sports free
of charge. All equipment is new to the opening of the center
and includes, stairmasters, bikes, ellipticals, treadmills, and erg
machines. There are several weight circuits, which have plate
and cable-loaded equipment, as well as free weights. Fitness
classes and personal training sessions are available for a small
fee. Visit *www.jhu.edu/~recsport* for more information.

Students Speak Out On...
Athletics

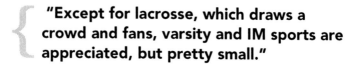

"Except for lacrosse, which draws a crowd and fans, varsity and IM sports are appreciated, but pretty small."

Q "**Lacrosse is pretty much the sport at Hopkins**. I'm from an area where football is big, so it was surprising to me that the crowds at lacrosse were so much bigger than those at football games. Homecoming is actually in the spring because that's lacrosse season."

Q "A lot of students don't really care about athletics. Many students don't exercise, and **IM sports are mostly frats and dorms**. A lot of students like lacrosse, but even with free tickets, the stadium doesn't fill up."

Q "If you're looking for a good football or basketball program, **look elsewhere**."

Q "We are Division III in all sports, except lacrosse. Lacrosse is very big at Hopkins, and everyone comes out for the games. Other than that, **sports are not huge on campus**, but many students do participate. IM sports are organized by specific groups, such as fraternities and dorms. They are present, but not huge. There are also club sports that meet about once a week, and are just fun for people who don't have time or aren't as serious as varsity players."

Q "Varsity sports, well all sports for that matter, aren't very big on campus. **We do well in lacrosse and baseball, but besides that, there's not a whole lot**. I know some people who participate in IM sports, and they enjoy it."

Q "**Hopkins men's lacrosse is big**, but that's the only Division I sport we have. Other than that, people sometimes watch the games, but they aren't a major deal. Lacrosse games are packed and way fun. IM sports aren't much of a deal, either, but are available to those who want them. My friends and I create our own pickup games when we want to play tennis."

Q "I'm on the varsity crew team. Lacrosse is huge, but I think they recruit for that. **There are a lot of IM opportunities**, and some teams that you could try out for even if you didn't participate in them at all in high school, like crew, for example."

Q "**People on varsity sports tend to stick together**. They are more high-profile than other people on campus, especially people on the lacrosse teams."

Q "Everyone comes out for the lacrosse games, and our homecoming is in the spring, during the season. There're also IM and club sports. **Club sports, such as lacrosse and soccer, are a lot of fun**. I know people who played both of those and loved it. They travel sometimes to other schools, but it's more relaxed, and they practice much less than varsity. Intramurals don't practice; there's a variety of sports to choose from, and anybody can join or form a team. A lot of dorms have teams—frats and sororities, and just groups of friends."

Q "The only big sport is really lacrosse. Our homecoming is in April for lacrosse, not football. **We have very little school spirit**, but lots of people are involved with intramurals."

Q **"Lacrosse is the number one sport on the campus** for both male and female teams. We are ranked number one in the country for it. In lacrosse, we are NCAA Division I, and all other sports we are NCAA Division III. Spirit and morale for other sports besides lacrosse is a little low. IM sports are pretty big, too, as long as you get your house or floormates involved in it. They can be a lot of fun."

Q "Lacrosse is huge, and the team is really good. The games we went to were tons of fun, because the whole student body really comes out. Other **sports are pretty poorly attended, and no one pays much attention**. You can definitely play IM sports with your hall, which is fun. Club sports, like ultimate, are another option if you want some more serious athletic involvement."

The College Prowler Take On...
Athletics

Athletics are not a major focus at Johns Hopkins. Even lacrosse, the most popular sport, doesn't bring out the whole student body. Tickets to events are free for students. Hopkins has one stadium, which is small by university standards. Homecoming is one of the few games where the stadium is filled. Students often are surprised that Hopkins celebrates Homecoming with a lacrosse game in the spring. Club and IM sports are open to everyone and aren't overly competitive. A relatively small number of students, however, participate in these events. At Hopkins, school spirit is defined by academics and research as opposed to athletics.

If you want a school with a strong athletics department, Hopkins is not the school for you. Hopkins makes up for its apathy in other sports with its support for lacrosse. Even so, some students do not care that the Hopkins lacrosse team is one of the top teams in the country. Other varsity sports are Division III, with low student support at games. There are many club and IM sports and a new recreation center if students want to stay active, but want less competition.

The College Prowler® Grade on

Athletics: B-

A high grade in Athletics indicates that students have school spirit, that sports programs are respected, that games are well-attended, and that intramurals are a prominent part of student life.

Nightlife

The Lowdown On...
Nightlife

Club and Bar Prowler:
Popular Nightlife Spots!

Club Prowler:

BAR Baltimore

Power Plant Live!

34 Market Place
Baltimore, MD

(410) 385-2992

www.powerplantlive.com

Bar Baltimore is located in the PowerPlant, the downtown club district. Thursday night is 18-and-over night.

Baja Beach Club

55 Market Place
Baltimore, MD

(410) 727-0468

Baja Beach Club has a full-blown beach theme both in terms of atmosphere and decor. Come early if you want a seat near the dance floor—this place is always crowded. Keep an eye out for hot waitresses in bikinis.

→

Have a Nice Day Café

Power Plant Live!
34 Market Place
Baltimore, MD
(410) 385-8869

www.haveanicedaybaltimore.com

Have a Nice Day Café is located at Power Plant Live! It is a tribute to different decades and is decorated with smiley faces and tie-dye. It's not as crowded as BAR Baltimore generally, and has a definite retro charm. The dancing area has lighting in the floor and the feel of a disco club, but the music is contemporary. Thursday night is 18 and over.

Bar Prowler:

The Brewer's Art

1106 N Charles St.
Baltimore, MD 21201
(410) 547-6925

www.belgianbeer.com

The Brewer's Art is located in a large, Mt. Vernon townhouse where they brew their own beer and provide a variety of very good, but highly-priced, dishes. The entire first floor is occupied by the upscale restaurant. Downstairs is the somewhat sketchier bar area, at least compared to the nice restaurant upstairs. Their home-made beers are pretty good.

Charles Village Pub

3107 St. Paul St.
Baltimore, MD 21218
(410) 243-1611

One of the most popular hangouts at Hopkins. It's one block from campus, has reasonable prices, and generally is showing a sports game or two on TV. The food is greasy, and exactly what someone would expect from a bar, especially one right next to a college campus. Many students go here for the appetizers as well as the drinks. The drinks are two for one during happy hour, from 4 p.m. to 6:30 p.m.

Greene Turtle

722 S Broadway
Baltimore, MD
(410) 342-4222

The Greene Turtle is a bar and eatery with multiple televisions and a pub-type atmosphere. The food is actually one of the focuses, and it's better than you'd normally expect from a bar. This is the type of place that kind of has two sections—one for diners and one for bar patrons. It's not a place where you generally see a whole lot of Hopkins students.

Howl at the Moon

Power Plant Live!
22 Market Place
Baltimore, MD

(410) 783-5111

www.howlatthemoon.com

Howl at the Moon is a bar with a unique theme. They have dueling pianos set up center stage, between the tables and the bar. A dance floor covers the space between the entrance and pianos. Early on, they can play some annoying stuff, but as the night progresses, they get a full band going and play some good stuff. They are also more than willing to take requests if the price is right.

PJ's Pub

3333 N Charles St.
Baltimore, MD

(410) 243-8844

A hole in the wall sort of place located right next to Wolman Hall, across the street from campus. Students who don't like Charles Village Pub often go to PJ's. Many students also order PJ's pizza. It's not great, but it's cheap, and since it's right next door, it's easy to do pickup and not have to tip for delivery. The TVs generally have sporting events on.

Spy Club

15 E Center St.
Baltimore, MD

(410) 685-4779

Spy Club is an upscale club located on the second and third floors of the Midtown Yacht Club. Serves dishes such as smoked salmon and paté for the more refined taste. They have an oxygen bar and admission is five dollars after 9:30 p.m. Sunday and Thursday nights are Britpop nights and they offer great tapas.

Other Places to Check Out:

Club Orpheus
Fraziers on the Avenue
Max's of Fell's Point
Red Maple

Bars Close At:
2 a.m., last call at 1:30 a.m.

Primary Areas with Nightlife:
Charles Village

Power Plant Live! at the Inner Harbor

Mount Vernon

Fell's Point

Canton

Student Favorites:
Charles Village Pub (CVP)

PJ's Pub

Cheapest Place to Get a Drink:
Charles Village Pub happy hour

Ruby Tuesday (buy a drink, get one for a penny)

Favorite Drinking Games:
Beer Pong (Beiruit)

Card Games (A$$hole)

Quarters

Power Hour

Useful Resources for Nightlife:
www.baltimoresun.com

www.marylandnightlife.com

What to Do if You're Not 21
Thursday nights are 18 and over at most clubs. Student groups offer organized trips to Baltimore clubs many Thursdays. Many bars, including PJ's and CVP, allow entry under 21 all the time. No one cards at frat parties or house parties. E-Level, in Levering Hall, has satellite television, video games, and a pool table.

Organization Parties
Many student organizations throw house parties. These parties are sponsored by individual upperclassmen members. These house parties offer an opportunity for students to get to know each other in a more social setting. Parties vary in size from a few students to approximately a hundred students.

Frats
See the Greek section!

Students Speak Out On...
Nightlife

{ **"CVP and PJ's are the two most popular bars next to campus. For clubs, you can go into Baltimore and find any type you're looking for."**

Q "Last year, the senior class officers organized a lot of good trips to clubs on Thursday nights. **There are a few bars near Hopkins, but no clubs**. Near the Inner Harbor, there are a lot of clubs with different themes. Howl at the Moon has dueling pianos, but it's better to go when there's a crowd. Bar of Baltimore is grungy and warehouse-like; they encourage girls to dance on the bar."

Q "Most **Hopkins students go to house parties** instead of clubs, and go dancing at clubs maybe once a month. Unless it's a Hopkins-sponsored event, more girls than guys go to clubs. They have lots of themed clubs and themed nights at clubs, including goth, techno, and gay nights. Clubbing is one of the few times you'll see people at Hopkins dressed up, but they're usually still more conservative than other patrons."

Q "The **school sponsors club night during orientation** at Have a Nice Day Café, which is a club, even though it doesn't sound like it. We had a big pre-lacrosse game party at a club called Baja. Both are in the Inner Harbor— about a 10-dollar cab ride away."

Q "There are not very many bars and clubs off campus. Mostly **there are fraternity parties**, and not much else. Downtown, by the Inner Harbor, there's more stuff to do."

"I love to dance and go to clubs, and I've found that Baltimore's clubs are pretty good. Often, once a month maybe, **a group at Hopkins will sponsor a club night and provide free transportation** with a reduced entry fee. Take advantage of these. These are really popular, and it's fun to see everyone out having fun! Sometimes the club is only Hopkins people, other times it's open to the public, as well. There is a bar called PJ's that is right next to the dorms, which is a lot of fun! There are also some classier bars that you can go to when you're actually 21, or want to hang with the older crowd. They are all tons of fun and offer a good variety!"

"There are two nearby: CVP and PJ's. These are within walking distance. **There's an area a cab ride away with a bunch of clubs and bars** where you pretty much just hop around between them. Everyone goes there for Halloween."

"**There are very cheesy clubs and bars at the Inner Harbor**. They tend to be dominated by a young crowd. My current favorite bar is a place called Red Maple on Charles Street. It's the closest that I've found to a Hollywood bar out here."

"Baltimore clubs suck, for the most part. If you're really into the whole club scene, **the best place to go is DC**. But if you don't mind average clubs, the one I like best is Bar Baltimore. As far as bars, most people go to CVP."

"The **best area to go for bars and clubs would be the Fell's Point area** in downtown Baltimore. It's about an eight-dollar cab ride from the University, so if you split it with a couple friends, it isn't too expensive. It's full of people from various colleges looking to have a good time."

Q "There are a lot of bars and clubs. Fell's Point, which has a row of bars down near the harbor, is really popular and fun. **There's another row of bars and clubs at a place called the Power Plant Live!** I like it there a lot! There are other clubs and bars scattered around the area, and of course, the local bar, PJ's."

Q "I don't go to bars, but I do love the clubs! Obviously, none compare to Miami Beach, where I'm from, **but there are a few good ones, especially on college nights**. I'd recommend Bar Baltimore, and Baja Beach Club. They're all good."

The College Prowler Take On...
Nightlife

Students like to go out to bars and clubs on the weekends. There are several bars near Hopkins, but no dance clubs within walking distance. Student organizations have realized the need for, and interest in, school-sponsored club nights. While groups used to organize these nights once a semester, they now offer them two to three times a month. For five dollars, students get transportation, club entry, and sometimes, drinks. Some of these nights are open only to Hopkins students, while others give students a chance to meet individuals from other schools. If students are willing to look around Baltimore, they will likely find a club that matches their interests. In addition, many students go to house parties with their friends.

Hopkins could use more bars and clubs in its immediate vicinity, but overall, students are not disappointed with nightlife options. There are often movies, plays, or concerts on campus, and club nights off campus. If students want to travel to the Inner Harbor or Fell's Point area, both of which are known for their nightlife, it is approximately a 10-dollar cab ride. For the few individuals who are unsatisfied with nightlife in Baltimore, students often ride together to Washington, DC for a night out.

The College Prowler® Grade on
Nightlife: B+

A high grade in Nightlife indicates that there are many bars and clubs in the area that are easily accessible and affordable. Other determining factors include the number of options for the under-21 crowd and the prevalence of house parties.

Greek Life

The Lowdown On...
Greek Life

Number of Fraternities: 13	**Undergrad Men in Fraternities:** 21%
Number of Sororities: 11	**Undergrad Women in Sororities:** 22%

→

Fraternities on Campus:

Alpha Delta Phi
Alpha Epsilon Pi
Alpha Phi Alpha
Beta Theta Pi
Lambda Phi Epsilon
Phi Gamma Delta
Phi Kappa Psi
Pi Kappa Alpha
Sigma Alpha Epsilon
Sigma Alpha Mu
Sigma Phi Epsilon
Sigma Chi

Sororities on Campus:

Alpha Kappa Alpha
Alpha Phi
Delta Sigma Theta
Kappa Alpha Theta
Kappa Kappa Gamma
Phi Mu
Sigma Gamma Rho

Other Greek Organizations:

Interfraternity Council
Panhellenic Council

Multicultural Colonies:

Alpha Kappa Delta Phi, sorority
Delta Xi Phi, sorority
Lambda Pi Chi, sorority
Lambda Upsilon Lambda, fraternity
Sigma Omicron Pi, sorority

Did You Know?

Freshmen aren't allowed to pledge a sorority or fraternity until second semester freshman year. This gives them an opportunity to develop a social life outside the Greek system.

Only one sorority, Phi Mu, has Greek housing, and their house is **operated under university housing**, complete with an RA.

Students Speak Out On...
Greek Life

{ **"Greek life doesn't necessarily dominate, but if you like to go out, you'll probably find yourself at frat parties. There's usually no cover for girls, and it's a good time. There's no need to join a frat or sorority to go to the parties."**

Q "When you're a freshman, **frat parties are the main place to go and hang out**. If you live in the AMRs, you're entire floor will probably traipse together to frats. However, most upperclassmen not in the Greek system attend private house parties. A lot of the time, girls can talk their way into not paying for entry to frat parties. Watch out for the punch. I once watched guys stir it with a broomstick lying around their basement."

Q "They exist, but they don't dominate the social scene, (except maybe freshman year). My roommate started to pledge and dropped out after he was accepted because it interfered with academics. **Even people in the Greek system put academics first**."

Q "A lot of people go to frat parties freshman year, and give it up thereafter. Some stay with it, but it's not a huge proportion. **Frats are generally more active**. Presently, only one sorority has its own house. Maryland law makes this difficult."

Q "Greek life is pretty minimal, though you'll always party at frat houses freshman year. **Everyone can go to the frat parties, but they get pretty sketchy** after a few months. Once you make friends with upperclassmen, there are private house parties everywhere."

Q "Greek life definitely does not dominate the scene at Hopkins. **About 30 percent of students participate**. You can be in a sorority or not be in one, and still know just as many people and the same people. Basically, I always say that frat parties, and Greek life in general, are there if you want them, but they're easy to ignore."

Q "It doesn't exactly dominate the social scene, but **frat parties are the usual hangout** for those with a more upbeat lifestyle—who like the fast, crazy, and wild weekend atmosphere. I'm in a sorority, but I can balance my life between my Greek and non-Greek friends. I usually end up spending more weekend time with my Greek friends just because they are more fun. They are the type to drink, go out to clubs and parties, dance, and enjoy life to its fullest."

Q "Greek life does not dominate the social scene, although it's part of the social scene. I have many friends who have never been to a frat party and many who frequent them. School is what you want it to be. There is no pressure to join a sorority; some of your friends will, but most won't. **Sororities don't have houses**, although they get around this by having occasional parties at members' houses. The commitment is more of a once-a-week meeting thing and you hang out together occasionally. You won't lose your friends to the Greek system, but it's there for you if you want it. I think it's a happy medium."

Q "I pledged as a sophomore, and until I did, I didn't realize just how large a role it played. As freshmen, we always hung out at the frats on Friday and Saturday nights, and sororities didn't seem that big. Then, after I joined one, I started hanging out with them a lot. It changed my social life at Hopkins drastically. It's a lot more social than I had thought the year before. **Hopkins is pretty much what you make of it**. You will always find people around that enjoy the same things as you do."

Q "Greek life tends to dominate the social scene for freshman. **Most people can't get off campus, so the easiest parties to get to are fraternity parties**. As the years go on, it depends on who your friends are and if they have cars. If they have cars, many people will go to clubs in DC. There'll be more to do once you get to know people better. Frats just serve as a way to get to know people in the beginning, and then you'll make friends and do whatever you want."

Q "I am not in a sorority, but all of my friends are. It just wasn't my thing. **I did rush and it was fun, but I'm just not a girly-type person**. You'll learn about them in your first semester and be able to make your decisions before rush second semester. Fraternities aren't bad, either. Some are more popular than others. I hang out with a lot of the fraternity guys. Groups are extremely distinguishable at Hopkins; it seems almost cliquey. Athletes basically hang out with athletes, and so on and so forth. That's not always the case, but a big majority of it is."

Q "Greek life is fun. **It definitely gives the campus life**. The fraternity parties are fun if you know which ones to go to, but it can never dominate the social scene. There are too many other things going on at the same time for them to dominate."

The College Prowler Take On...
Greek Life

Students agree that Greek life plays a presence in campus life, but it does not dominate the social scene. There are several reasons for this. Students cannot pledge their first semester freshmen year, so they are forced to make friends outside their fraternity or sorority. Even sophomore year, very few people live in Greek-sponsored housing. Guys in most fraternities have the opportunity to live in a frat house, but only one sorority provides housing. For those not in the Greek system, frat parties play a large role in freshmen social life, but not so much thereafter. There is a lot of interaction between people who are part of the Greek system and those who are not.

Approximately one fifth of the student population is a member of a fraternity or sorority. Those within the Greek system claim to be satisfied with the level of involvement expected, but the requirements are less intense than other schools. Academics co-exist with Greek life. For those students who want a school with a strong Greek system, they might be less happy with Hopkins' Greek system. People who don't want to be a part of Greek life can find many other opportunities for social interaction, but for those who want the friendship and support of Greek life, Hopkins offers many different fraternities and sororities.

The College Prowler® Grade on

Greek Life: B+

A high grade in Greek Life indicates that sororities and fraternities are not only present, but also active on campus. Other determining factors include the variety of houses available and the respect the Greek community receives from the rest of the campus.

Drug Scene

The Lowdown On...
Drug Scene

Most Prevalent Drugs on Campus:
Ecstasy
Marijuana
Ritalin/Caffeine Pills

Liquor-Related Referrals:
285

Liquor-Related Arrests:
0

Drug-Related Referrals:
25

Drug-Related Arrests:
0

Drug Counseling Programs:
Free, confidential drug and alcohol counseling.
(410) 516-8278 between 8:30 a.m.–5 p.m.

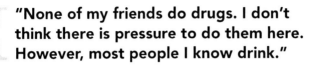
Students Speak Out On...
Drug Scene

"None of my friends do drugs. I don't think there is pressure to do them here. However, most people I know drink."

Q "**I've never come across any drugs on campus**, except for marijuana. My roommate smoked every couple of weeks, and he never got busted, even though our room smelled like smoke."

Q "There is **some drug use**, but it is relatively low-key."

Q "Some people use drugs, but **you don't really come across them very often unless you're looking for them**. People who want to use don't seem to have trouble finding what they're looking for, but there's no pressure either way."

Q "As with any college, there are definitely drugs and alcohol available on campus. They are especially rampant at frat parties. It all depends on where you choose to go and who you choose to associate with. The most important thing, though, is that **no one is pressuring you to do anything at Hopkins**, which I found to be the best part. People are very understanding and considerate."

Q "Drugs are there if you want them, but **they're not everywhere**. I don't do drugs, and it doesn't bother me."

Q "**The drug scene seems pretty small**—nothing hardcore or excessive."

Q "I haven't encountered any hard drug use. Some students smoke pot. Alcohol use is prevalent. Almost everyone drinks. Moreover, **people drink to get drunk**. No cocktails at Hopkins, just shots of cheap vodka."

Q "I don't think there are many drugs on campus, but I'm not into that. I'm sure you can get them if you want them, and there are people that do. I think **for the most part, alcohol is most prevalent**. But if you don't want to take part in it, you can still go to a party and enjoy yourself with no questions asked."

Q "Drugs are not that big here. **Alcohol continues to be the substance of choice**."

Q "**If you are looking for it, you can find it**. It's here, though not everywhere. There is one frat known for its pot-smoking antics."

Q "**Hopkins has a fair amount of pot**. I don't smoke, so I don't know the details. Some other drugs are available, too."

The College Prowler Take On...
Drug Scene

The consensus among students is that you can find drugs on campus if you want them, but they are not overwhelmingly present. Alcohol is the top drug used on campus, followed by pot. Students also use caffeine pills and other drugs that help them stay awake. In this case, students use these drugs not to escape the world, but because they need to study. The best aspect of the drug scene at Hopkins, however, is that there is no pressure to use drugs at Hopkins. Students are understanding about letting other students make their own choices about drug and alcohol use (and abuse).

Drug use at Hopkins is a matter of choice. It is very uncommon to hear about anyone allowing their drug or alcohol use to interfere with their studies. When people choose to use drugs, it is usually on the weekends as a chance to relax. Even where drugs are used, they are not a visible presence on campus because there isn't pressure from others to use.

A-

The College Prowler® Grade on

Drug Scene: A-

A high grade in the Drug Scene indicates that drugs are not a noticeable part of campus life; drug use is not visible, and no pressure to use them seems to exist.

Campus Strictness

The Lowdown On...
Campus Strictness

What Are You Most Likely to Get Caught Doing on Campus?

- Drinking outside or in common areas of dorms.

- Downloading copyrighted material from the network.

- Being present at a party broken up for noise violations.

- Parking on campus without a permit.

- Bringing food or drink into the MSE or computer labs.

Students Speak Out On...
Campus Strictness

"Campus police are meant to protect you, not arrest you. I don't know anyone who has gotten expelled for drinking. The worst thing they do is call your parents if an RA writes you up, but RAs are lenient."

Q "**Common sense is the main rule to follow here**. Don't openly drink in the dorms or on campus. Some people do drink in their rooms and get away with it, but Hopkins's official policy is that it's not allowed. So don't challenge your RA to a drinking contest or put alcohol in a water bottle and think no one will notice."

Q "Even if you get busted, **if you show any signs that you are sorry, you won't get thrown out of the dorms**; (unless you're violent, in which case they will throw out immediately.) There are usually only a couple of people thrown out of housing each year, although everyone seems to be on probation. Hop Cops generally want to help you, and they want you to stay safe. Unless they think you're a danger, they won't bust you."

Q "There is a no tolerance policy about drugs and drinking, so obviously it is taken very seriously. But **as long as you are not rowdy or disruptive, you'll usually be okay**."

Q "**Police try to be strict on alcohol and drugs**; neither is allowed on campus. The deans are pretty tough about it. If you are caught, they call your parents."

Q "They're fairly strict, but **people still drink like fish here**."

Q "**Hop Cops are around to keep us Hopkins students out of the hands of Baltimore police**, and protect Hopkins's reputation."

Q "If you are caught with drugs, you can get kicked on the first offense. For drinking, you mostly just get warnings from RAs and Hop Cops, but **after your third offense, you are out**."

Q "**Sometimes police are strict, and sometimes they're not. Don't get caught in your dorm drinking**, or you will get probation. However, you won't get caught unless your RA finds out. Frat parties sometimes get broken up, but no one gets into trouble, and major parties never get broken up. Drinking and drugs do go on and police don't do a whole lot about it. So, just don't do it in the open. You don't even have to drink, though. I have friends that never drank, and some that did often. It's college—you are treated as an adult and held responsible."

Q "Campus is supposed to be dry. So, how often you get busted really depends on your RA. They do have substance-free housing, but you could still get an RA that doesn't care if you party in your room, or you could get an RA that will bust you if you're being loud after coming back from a party. So, **be intelligent about drinking** or whatever, and it usually isn't a problem."

Q "**There is also a strict Honor Code** they are starting to crack down on now. Cheating was considered a widespread problem, and they are tightening down on it. If you get caught, it could be anything from failing the class to being expelled from the University. So, just don't get caught."

Q "Don't sweat the Hop Cops—you can always just run from them. RAs are sometimes really strict, but it depends on their mood. **You can always find someplace to drink** if you have friends, and there seems to be a drug subculture, at least a little."

The College Prowler Take On...
Campus Strictness

Everyone agrees that you can minimize your chances of getting caught by not drinking or doing drugs in dorm common areas or outside. It's also a good idea to keep all parties in the dorms quiet and keep doors shut. RAs have the power to give warnings for drugs or alcohol. Although the school claims to have a no-tolerance policy, students generally get three warnings before being thrown out. (Be aware, however, that since drinking in the dorms is forbidden, anyone caught in a room where people are drinking will receive an alcohol warning. If you are worried that someone may be in danger due to substance abuse, however, do not be afraid to call HERO or your RA. They care more about people's well-being than about issuing warnings.) Hop Cops want to help students stay safe. Although they can arrest students who are violent or rowdy, they don't usually do so. As one student pointed out, campus does have an ethics committee that enforces infractions for plagiarism. They are very strict. For substance infractions, if you don't flaunt that you are breaking the rules, you are unlikely to get in trouble.

Campus strictness is not really an issue. People do get caught, but there are very seldom serious consequences to infractions. When there are consequences, they may range from having your parents called to being expelled from housing, or being expelled from Hopkins. In most circumstances, the consequences are not great enough to deter students from breaking rules. They just need to remember to use caution.

The College Prowler® Grade on

Campus
Strictness: B-

A high Campus Strictness grade implies an overall lenient atmosphere; police and RAs are fairly tolerant, and the administration's rules are flexible.

Parking

The Lowdown On...
Parking

JHU Parking Services
(410) 516-7275

Student Parking Lot?
No

**Freshmen Allowed
to Park?**
No

Parking Permits:

Baltimore City
Parking Authority

200 W Lombard St., Suite B
Baltimore, MD 21201

(443) 573-2800

Fax: (410) 685-1557

E-Mail: parkingauthority@bcp
arking.com

Web Site: *www.ci.baltimore.
md.us/government/parking*

→

Common Parking Tickets:

Expired Meter: $20

No-Parking Zone: $20

Fire Lane: $32

Parking in a Residential Zone (for more than two hours): $27

Handicapped Zone: $202

Did You Know?

Best Places to Find a Parking Spot
St. Paul St., 29th St.

Good Luck Getting a Parking Spot Here
34th St. between Wolman and McCoy

Students Speak Out On...
Parking

"Parking is one thing that sucks at Hopkins. Freshmen and sophomores are not allowed to have cars. The upperclassmen that do have cars have a hard time finding places to park."

Q "**On-campus parking for students is almost nonexistent**. However, if you're dedicated and creative, you can usually find parking within a few blocks. Charles and St. Paul are both good places to look for spots, although they have bizarre rules about when you can and cannot park on them. University is your best bet because you can leave your car there for weeks on end, but good luck finding a spot unless you have a compact car. Look on 29th Street, which also has 24-hour parking, but it's a bit farther from campus."

Q "Freshman and sophomores should use meter parking because it's cheaper than a garage. If you live in a row-house junior or senior year, pay 20 dollars to get a residential parking permit. Otherwise, **you can only park for two hours near your house**."

Q "Well, **you're not supposed to have a car as a freshman, but some people do it**. It's completely unnecessary to have one, so I wouldn't even bother searching for a parking spot for it. There are shuttles and cabs that serve whatever you'd need."

Q "There is parking, although **you may have to walk far**. It's not easy to park, but it's possible to find good spots."

Q "There is **no parking for undergraduates** at all, unless you are commuting from home."

Q "Not many students bring cars before their junior year because it's not necessary. There are taxis, buses, and the rail system for going to the airport and Washington. **Cars are nice, but it's Baltimore—you don't need one**, and you are going to have to find parking. Hopkins has two main student lots: one on campus and one off campus. The one off campus is a couple blocks away, and the wait list is a year for it. For the one on campus, you have to live a quarter of a mile away from campus and get a permit. There is street parking, but it's a hassle to find. Don't worry about having a car."

Q "**The parking scene is pretty bad**, being in the city. You can find spaces, but it is hard."

Q "Parking is a bit of a hassle. I wouldn't recommend bringing a car just because it's not really necessary. Most things are within walking distance, or you can take a cab, **ride a shuttle, or take public transportation**. You can find visitor parking on the streets. As a student, you have to get special permission to park on campus, and it gets annoying when you're constantly being ticketed."

Q "Most **people don't have cars until maybe sophomore year, at the earliest**. You really don't need a car to get to classes because it's such a small campus. But as far as parking, some people park in campus lots and keep their cars there, while others get parking permits once they move off campus. The farthest most people will live off campus is maybe a 15-minute walk. No one really needs a car to get to classes—it's more of a convenience and enjoyment thing. Parking can be tight for sophomores, and even more so for freshmen."

Q "**Parking is slightly difficult**, but not impossible. You can rent your own garage for very cheap."

Q "Parking is **almost near to impossible**. Don't bring a car unless you are sure you have a place to park."

Q "Parking stinks. **There is nothing on campus unless you get a pass, and still, it's not very good**. Off campus, you deal with the city of Baltimore, and you can't get a pass until you move out of the dorms and have a 'permanent residence.' It's annoying, but I've had a car here since my sophomore year; you make do."

Q "I hear parking is a pain. **You don't need a car, anyway**. The most I did outside of campus was to go to the movies or go to a club sponsored by the college and they provided the transportation. You can always take a taxi, and the college shuttle takes you as far as a mile from the campus for free, back and forth. It's more of a hassle than anything else your first year."

The College Prowler Take On...
Parking

Students are generally disappointed with the lack of parking on or near campus. Although there is talk of building a new garage for student parking, one does not exist presently. Commuter students can buy parking permits to park on campus, but only one percent of undergraduates commute. Students disagree over the importance of bringing a car. Those who do choose to bring a car will need to plan to spend time feeding meters, moving their cars from no parking zones, and simply finding a spot. Because apartments and many row-houses do not have parking, students compete with residents of Charles Village for parking. If you live in a row-house, you can buy a parking permit and park near your house with no trouble. (If the car is not in your name, however, you must bring a notarized letter from the owner saying that you are the primary driver. In addition, you must bring a copy of your lease to the parking authority.)

Parking, specifically for students, is virtually nonexistent. Students can find parking by searching the streets near Hopkins. If worse comes to worse, you can always find a spot within a mile of campus, from which you will have to move your car in two hours. It is not necessary to have a car to get around campus, so once students find parking spots, they keep them until they need to drive somewhere else in the city. If you're flexible about where you park, you'll find parking, even if it isn't near where you want to go.

The College Prowler® Grade on

Parking: D-

A high grade in this section indicates that parking is both available and affordable, and that parking enforcement isn't overly severe.

Transportation

The Lowdown On...
Transportation

Ways to Get Around Town:

On Campus
Hopkins Security escort van
(410) 516-8700
5 p.m.–3 a.m., drives anywhere within a mile radius of campus

Homewood/East Baltimore Medical Campus Shuttle
(410) 516-4600
6:30 a.m.–11 p.m., connects Shriver Hall at Homewood with Penn Station, Peabody/ Mount Vernon, and the Medical School

Public Transportation
Maryland Transit Authority (MTA)
(410) 539-5000

The bus stops on Charles St. heading north, and St. Paul St. heading south. The fare is $1.35. Check out *www.mtamaryland.com*.

The light rail and subway have tracks through Baltimore. There have been talks about expanding the system, but nothing has materialized.

→

(Public Transportation, continued)

Since neither of these transportation systems passes near the Homewood campus, students do not often use the light rail or subway systems. One-way fare is $1.60, or a day pass is $3.50. Check www.mtamaryland.com for more information and schedules.

Taxi Cabs

Checker's
(410) 685-1212

Northern Cab
(410) 668-9400

Royal
(410) 327-0330

Sedan Transport
(410) 719-2222

Sun
(410) 235-0300

Yellow
(410) 792-4005

Car Rentals

Alamo, local: (410) 850-5011
national: (800) 327-9633
www.alamo.com

Avis, local: (410) 859-1680
national: (800) 831-2847
www.avis.com

Budget, local: (410) 859-0850
national: (800) 527-0700
www.budget.com

Dollar, local: (410) 859-5600
national: (800) 800-4000
www.dollar.com

(Car Rentals, continued)

Enterprise,
national: (800) 736-8222
www.enterprise.com

Hertz, local: (410) 850-7400
national: (800) 654-3131
www.hertz.com

National, local: (410) 859-8860
national: (800) 227-7368
www.nationalcar.com

Best Ways to Get Around Town

Find a friend with a car

Hopkins and Colltown Shuttle Service

Taxi

Ways to Get Out of Town:

Airport

Baltimore Washington International (BWI) Airport

(410) 859-7111

BWI Airport is approximately 30-minutes driving time from Johns Hopkins.

Airlines Serving Baltimore

American Airlines
(800) 433-7300,
www.aa.com

Continental (800) 523-3273,
www.continental.com

(Airlines, continued)

Delta, (800) 221-1212
www.delta.com

Northwest, (800) 225-2525
www.nwa.com

Southwest, (800) 435-9792
www.southwest.com

TWA, (800) 221-2000
www.twa.com

United, (800) 241-6522
www.united.com

US Airways, (800) 428-4322
www.usairways.com

How to Get to the Airport

Go south on Charles St. past Art Museum Dr.

Follow it around to the right, around the Wyman Dell onto 29th St.

Take 29th St. to the second right, and merge onto Howard St.

Continue on Howard St. as it merges into Martin Luther King Blvd.

Follow the signs to I-295.

Take I-295 South for approximately 10 miles.

Follow the signs and get off at I-195, and take the road east to the airport terminal.

A cab ride to the airport costs approximately $30.

Greyhound

210 W Fayette St.
www.greyhound.com
(800) 229-9424

The Greyhound bus terminal is located in downtown Baltimore, approximately three miles from campus.

Amtrak

Penn Station
1525 N Charles St.
(410) 291-4268
www.amtrak.com

Penn Station is located on the shuttle route, approximately one and one-half miles from campus. For schedule information, call (800) USA-RAIL.

The MARC train is the commuter section of Amtrak. It leaves from Penn Station and connects Baltimore to Washington, DC. A roundtrip ticket to Washington, DC costs approximately $11, but the trains only run on weekdays. For schedule information, call (410) 539-5000.

www.mtamaryland.com/marc/marc.asp

Travel Agents

Council Travel
Gilman Hall Book Center
(410) 516-0560
www.sta.travel.com

Students Speak Out On...
Transportation

"There's lots of good public transportation around Baltimore, especially between universities. The MARC train to DC is a nice and affordable, but unfortunately, it doesn't travel on weekends."

Q "**The Hopkins's shuttle system is a really nice, safe way to get around** within a mile of campus. It's also easy to get to Towson with the Colltown shuttle to go to the mall or to the movies. If you want to go anywhere else in town, however, you basically have to take a cab because the bus system is slow, and there's virtually no subway system."

Q "Everyone uses the shuttle service, but I don't think a lot of people use the bus system. Almost everyone knows someone who has a car and can take them places, and besides, **there's nowhere you really need to go that's not within a mile of campus**. I think more people might use the subway if it actually went anywhere, but it's rumored to only have a few stops."

Q "We take cabs, mostly. There's also the light rail and a campus shuttle that runs to Penn Station. **There are also shuttles to grocery stores**, Blockbuster, and the mall—all free of course."

Q "**There are always cabs available**, which are convenient to take to the Harbor and Fell's Point. There are also MTA buses, which are cheaper, although a little sketchier. I hear they are very convenient and reliable."

Q "Cabs are everywhere, but **the bus system is kind of sketchy**. Just like any big city, you'll find all kinds of people on the buses. Imagine NY buses, but less numbers of people on each bus."

Q "If you want to take Amtrak or the MARC, **there is a free shuttle from Hopkins that takes you to the station** pretty easily. I've taken it a few times. You can also take a five dollar taxi there. Taxis are pretty easy to catch near campus, so that's not a problem. There is also a free shuttle to the mall. The campus security van will take you within a mile for free—I take that all the time."

Q "**Public transportation sucks**, but the schools have a shuttle service that lets you get from school to school for free."

Q "Public **transportation is easy to use**. There are always cabs nearby, and the buses are cheap and can get you pretty far. There are shuttles that go to the train station, and from there you can take the train to DC on a weekday for $5.75 if you use the MARC train. There are also free shuttles to the Peabody Music Conservatory, Hopkins Medical School, and one of the malls in the area."

Q "I don't take buses, or anything like that. If you need to get out, **you can usually walk, take a shuttle, or call a taxi**. There's really no need for buses. Everything you'd need is right here."

The College Prowler Take On...
Transportation

Many students do not find a need to use Baltimore City public transportation. They use shuttle services geared towards college students, which can get them to the Harbor, the Hopkins Medical School, Peabody Conservatory of Music, Towson, the mall, other area universities, and anywhere within a mile of campus. When students want to go to DC, they take a shuttle to Penn Station and take the Amtrak or MARC trains. When students do use the city's public transportation, they find that it is reliable and cheap, even though it may be "sketchy."

Baltimore public transportation isn't great, but it will suffice. The main complaint about Baltimore public transportation is that many connections to reach different points in the city cannot be made easily. There are also entire sections of the city and suburbs that are not accessible by public transportation. Some students feel unsafe on the buses because of the mix of individuals who use them for travel. Almost anywhere students need to go can, however, be accessed by private University shuttles. Since many students do not have cars, they use mostly shuttle services and taxis to get around Baltimore. Students don't generally cite lack of public transportation as a reason that they don't leave the Homewood campus.

The College Prowler® Grade on
Transportation: B+

A high grade for Transportation indicates that campus buses, public buses, cabs, and rental cars are readily-available and affordable. Other determining factors include proximity to an airport and the necessity of transportation.

Weather

The Lowdown On...
Weather

Average Temperature:

Fall: 61°F
Winter: 38°F
Spring: 58°F
Summer: 80°F

Average Precipitation:

Fall: 3.2 in.
Winter: 3.0 in.
Spring: 3.5 in.
Summer: 3.7 in.

Students Speak Out On...
Weather

"Summers get pretty hot. Winters are fairly mild, although there's usually at least one substantial snowfall. Campus can get pretty muddy, so bring at least one pair of sturdy shoes."

Q "Bring clothing for all seasons, although **it doesn't usually stay extremely cold for very long**. The weather in Baltimore is really weird; storms frequently come up quickly in the evenings. All in all, it's not too bad. It's almost never over 100 degrees or under 30 degrees. The one thing you might want, though, is air-conditioning or a good fan."

Q "Baltimore **weather is unpredictable**. Have clothing available for all different weather."

Q "It is sort of warm. **We don't get a lot of snow**, but we do get it. Chances are, you'll be home for intersession then, though. You'll need a jacket, but not one that's good to -50 degrees, like the one I used at home."

Q "Baltimore is hot in September and cold in January. It doesn't snow much, but **it's very humid in August and September**."

Q "The weather in **Baltimore is typically warm and cold during the appropriate seasons** and not very extreme. It is pretty rainy in the spring, but other than that, it's not too bad. This past year, though, was a little more variable."

Q "**The weather is about 10 degrees warmer than in NY**, where I am from, but it has snowed. It doesn't rain often, and on most days it's sunny."

Q "Weather is random, very random. **In the dorms, it's always 80 degrees** and people wear shorts, but outside it can get cold. I grew up in CA and thought it was cold here, and that was before the snow season."

Q "The **weather was really nice this year**. I was at school for intersession, and it only snowed once. It was pretty windy this spring, but that's my only complaint."

Q "**It could look nice outside and still be cold**, and it could rain but still be warm. When it rains, it's normally humid, so I guess that's one way you can tell if it will rain. It can get very warm in the summers due to humidity."

Q "Weather was awesome this year. It was pretty mild. It only snowed once in January. I'm from Michigan originally, so it was a little adjustment. Most of the year, **the temperature ranged between the 50s and 70s**, with a couple weeks when it was warmer, and a few when it was cooler."

Q "For the first semester, it was beautiful with very little rain. It is kind of windy, but not too bad. **It never got really bitter cold**, with only one day of snow. It was 50 to 70 degrees pretty much constantly after February, with the exception of one really hot week in April."

The College Prowler Take On...
Weather

The weather is unpredictable in Baltimore. Students from the north tend to complain that it never gets really cold, and that it hardly ever snows. There are usually several small snowfalls each winter, but the city shuts down because it isn't prepared to deal with snow. (Although public schools close at the hint of snow, Johns Hopkins stays open at long as possible because it is so difficult to reschedule classes. When Hopkins does cancel class, most professors reschedule classes at their convenience.) It is sunny on most days, but storms come up without warning. It is not uncommon to have thunderstorms every night during the spring and summer. Bring clothing for a variety of seasons.

Most students don't find the weather in Baltimore unpleasant. They do, however, dislike not knowing what kind of weather to expect at any given time. Many days it looks warm outside while it is still cold and windy. People who stay at Hopkins during the summer complain about the humidity, but during the school year, the weather is overall mild. As long as you are prepared for unpredictable weather, Baltimore weather should not be a detriment to enjoying life at Hopkins.

The College Prowler® Grade on

Weather: B-

A high Weather grade designates that temperatures are mild and rarely reach extremes, that the campus tends to be sunny rather than rainy, and that weather is fairly consistent rather than unpredictable.

Report Card Summary

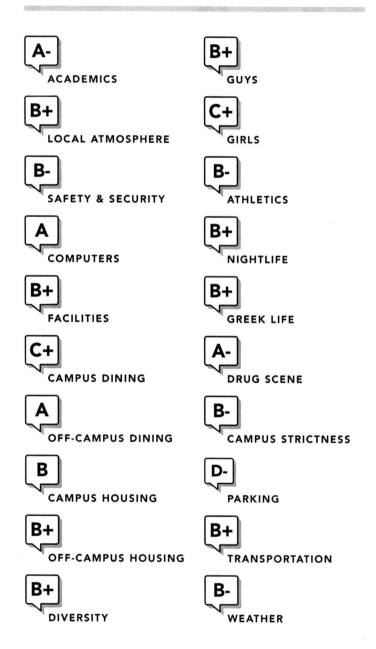

A- ACADEMICS

B+ LOCAL ATMOSPHERE

B- SAFETY & SECURITY

A COMPUTERS

B+ FACILITIES

C+ CAMPUS DINING

A OFF-CAMPUS DINING

B CAMPUS HOUSING

B+ OFF-CAMPUS HOUSING

B+ DIVERSITY

B+ GUYS

C+ GIRLS

B- ATHLETICS

B+ NIGHTLIFE

B+ GREEK LIFE

A- DRUG SCENE

B- CAMPUS STRICTNESS

D- PARKING

B+ TRANSPORTATION

B- WEATHER

Overall Experience

Students Speak Out On...
Overall Experience

"I appreciated the challenge. I enjoyed the fact that I actually had to work to succeed here. This is a great place for some people, but it's not for everyone. I would definitely come back here."

"I really like Hopkins. For me, **it's a good balance of liberal and conservative views**. I think that I'm getting a great education and that students are really working to make the overall social experience better. I still kind of wish that more students at Hopkins got excited about the school. I think that they don't appreciate the opportunities here. I sometimes feel that way about the professors, also."

Q "Naturally, there are things I've liked and things I haven't, but overall, **I've had a good experience**, and I'm glad I came."

Q "My experience has been great. **I love Hopkins**."

Q "Overall, I think I had a good college experience at Hopkins. **I was pushed to my limits and was challenged in many ways**, and I think I came out a better person for it. I often wondered what it would have been like had I gone to a different school."

Q "**Hopkins provides incredible opportunities to undergraduates** that aren't possible at other institutions, especially in research. Socially, it's what you make of it. There's a lot going on, but it's not force-fed to you the way it is at some other schools."

Q "Basically, if you're going to college for a well-rounded social experience, then Hopkins may not be the place. It is **very academically driven**, with many focused and hard-working students. You can find social life through sororities, and Hopkins gives you great resources, especially if you're pre-med or pre-law. But think twice if you want to have fun and have good grades at the same time. Hopkins is grade-deflated, and you must work hard for a good GPA. Otherwise, you meet life-changing friends, develop great relationships, and understand what it means to grow up and become a focused person."

Q "**Most of the people are cutthroat**, but you'll also find the sweetest and nicest people. Don't get me wrong, I'm a BME. You do a lot of studying. Your first semester is pass/fail, so you don't get any grades, which was good. Overall, I think it depends on your major and what you ultimately want to be."

Q "**I love it a lot, but I'm a bit of a geek**. I'm not afraid to admit it. It's very challenging, and the people are nice. I don't really have any complaints."

Q "At Hopkins, **we study hard and play hard**! There is a ton of stuff to do in Baltimore. I think that it is a difficult school, but I am having a wonderful time, and I think that I am doing really well. The people are awesome— most of the kids are middle class and aren't showy or pretentious—one reason why I chose JHU over Yale or Harvard. I can't picture myself anywhere else."

Q "I really like it at Hopkins. My friends are the best I could ever ask for. We really enjoy ourselves on the weekends. I only wish it was easier to get good grades. **The grading is very harsh**. Only a small percentage of each class receives an A. If it wasn't for the fact that I'm a pre-med, I wouldn't care too much. But I must be careful that my grades aren't too low."

Q "I'm pretty happy with the Hopkins scene. It's definitely not for everyone, but **everyone makes what they want out of their college experience**. I joined an a capella group, and several other rewarding clubs. I think Hopkins was probably the best choice for me."

Q "I love Hopkins. I complain about it all the time, but it's really been the best, yet most challenging, experience I've ever had. **Some keys to success at Hopkins: time management, love your major, love your friends**, and have some fun."

The College Prowler Take On...
Overall Experience

Students who love Hopkins and students who hate it both recognize that it isn't the school for everyone. Many students wish that Hopkins offered grade inflation, as other top schools do. Even people who work hard end up with low grades. This encourages some students to put studying above any social activity in hopes of being one of several people in a class who receives an "A." Hopkins offers a variety of social programming, but no one forces students to participate. There's no one holding your hand and leading you to fun activities. Even though students complain, most say that they've enjoyed being challenged by their experiences at Hopkins.

Hopkins presents a well-rounded experience for some students, but not every student takes advantage of the academic, social, and extracurricular opportunities. Some students wish that Hopkins encouraged students to get involved in all aspects of University life, but once you realize that it doesn't, you can make your own choices about how you want to spend your time. Academics and facilities are strong points at Hopkins. While on-campus dining and nightlife have not been strong points in the past, the administration is presently putting time and money into improving these aspects of University life.

The Inside Scoop

The Lowdown On...
The Inside Scoop

JHU Slang:

Know the slang, know the school. The following is a list of things you really need to know before coming to JHU. The more of these words you know, the better off you'll be.

AC – Athletic Center.

BME – Bio-medical engineering.

Cutthroat – Sabotaging other people's assignments to get ahead in class.

DSAGA – Diverse Sexuality and Gender Alliance.

E-level – Snack bar and social lounge in Levering Hall.

Glass Pav – Glass pavilion in Levering Hall. Used mainly for assemblies.

HAC Lab – The main computer lab on campus.

HERO – Hopkins's emergency response unit.

Hop Cops – Hopkins security officers.

HOPSFA – The Hopkins science fiction club.

➡

The HUT – Hutzler Undergraduate Library. An all-night study room on the second floor of Gilman Hall.

IAP – Introduction to American Politics class.

IFC – Inter-faith center.

IFP – Introduction to Fiction and Poetry class.

Meal Equiv – Meal Equivalency; when you trade in a meal on the meal plan for à la carte items.

MSE – Milton S. Eisenhower Library, the main library on campus.

SAIS – School of Advanced International Studies.

Things I Wish I Knew Before Coming to JHU

• Many people arrive planning to have a bad experience because they have absolutely no desire to attend Hopkins. They only ended up at Hopkins as a fall back.

• There's no substitute for the social atmosphere of the AMRs freshman year.

• Choose courses that look good, not courses that look like they are geared towards freshmen. If you end up in over your head, you can drop the course. Remember that first semester courses are pass/fail.

• Apply for a Wilson Fellowship, even if you don't feel like you have a perfect idea. Advisors let you change your topic at any point. It's an incredible opportunity to travel and do independent research. The fellowships are given to both humanities and science students, so don't feel like it needs to be a new breakthrough in research. In the past years, one person made a film, another examined landmine detection technology, and a third discussed spiritual practices of world religious leaders.

Tips to Succeed at JHU

- Go to your professors' office hours and get to know them before the end of the semester.

- Don't load up on all of your distribution credits in one semester.

- Don't count on being able to study in your room. If you can, great, but most people find a study room or library floor that they like best.

- Keep at least a little money in your J-Cash account. It's a pain when you have to go back to your room for printing, copying, or a soda.

- If you feel stressed, work out at the Recreation Center, go to the counseling center, or get a little sleep. Hopkins has many facilities ready to help unhappy students.

JHU Urban Legends

- One of the dining halls was shut down for 14 health violations, including having rat droppings in the food-preparation area. The most disturbing aspect of this legend is that it's true—ask upperclassmen if they remember when it happened.

- Supposedly there are hidden labs underneath Bloomberg, the physics building, where secret government experiments are conducted. In addition, there's a room in the building with a smaller than normal door set about a foot off the floor with a sign that claims it is the Monopole Storage Room. (A monopole should be impossible to create or store.) Graduate students become extremely evasive when asked about it.

- Students claim that there is a set of underground steam tunnels that link the basements of various buildings on campus.

School Spirit

Overall, students at Hopkins are not particularly spirited. There are some events, however, that students get excited about. The only sport that warrants student excitement is lacrosse. The activity that sparks the most interest is a capella, with the singing groups frequently performing to standing-room-only crowds. Students also get very spirited about their majors, often comparing themselves favorably to equivalent majors at other schools. School spirit drops off noticeably during exam time, when students lose interest in almost everything but their studies.

Traditions

No one can walk across the University seal located in the main entrance to Gilman Hall. Tradition says that if they are a prospective student, they won't be admitted to Hopkins. If they are an undergraduate, they will not graduate.

Every semester during finals, the Outdoor Society runs naked through the main campus library one evening to break the monotony and seriousness of studying.

Spring Fair is held every April. It is the one event that draws almost every student from Hopkins outside. There is a concert by a national act, student plays, and student musical performances. Craft vendors come from around the Mid-Atlantic area, and student groups sell goods or services. In addition, the beer garden is popular with students who are 21 years old or older.

Finding a Job or Internship

The Lowdown On...
Finding a Job or Internship

The Career Center offers many services to students, but students commonly complain that career counselors are only interested in helping students who know which field they want to enter; have an idea of what you are interested in before meeting with a counselor. Because Hopkins has so many successful alumni, don't forget that networking with them is a great way to get an internship or job.

Advice

Go to the Career Center first semester to beat the crowd when trying to find out about summer internships.

Use HopkinsNET to network with alumni about a summer internship. (In order to intern for credit, you must make no more than a minimal stipend from the position.)

Although Career Fairs are held on the Recreation Center basketball courts, don't forget to wear business attire, and bring many copies of your resumé.

Career Center Resources & Services

Workshops and Classes – "Resumés and Cover Letters," "Interviewing," "How to Work a Job Fair," "Breaking into Law," "Creating a CV for the Academic Job Search," "Applying to Graduate School," and "Creating your Job Search Plan."

HopkinsNET – Students can network with the thousands of alumni who post their information on this server.

Career Center Library – Books, directories, and periodicals to help you define your career goals, find a job or internship, and prepare for interviews. This is a non-circulating library.

Career Fairs – Graduate School Fair, General, Public Service, and Bioscience/Health Career Fairs.

E-Newsletter – Weekly *Job and Internship Opportunities Newsletter*.

Intersession Trips – Designed to help students learn about careers in a particular field, such as communications, film, and Wall Street in New York City; and law, politics, and biotechnology in Washington, DC.

On-Campus Recruiting – Employers come to Hopkins to interview students who have put their resumés in the on-campus recruiting database.

Peer Counselors – Answer general questions about searching for a job and critique resumés.

Staff Counselors – Administer and explain career-interest surveys, and help students decide on a career path.

Firms That Most Frequently Hire Grads

American Management Systems (AMS), Citigroup Corporate and Investment Bank (SSMB), Lehman Brothers, Medtronic, and National Security Agency (NSA)

Grads Who Enter the Job Market Within

6 Months: 45%
1 Year: 68%

Alumni

The Lowdown On...
Alumni

Web Site:
http://webapps.jhu.edu/
jhuniverse/alumni/

Office:
Steinwald House
3211 N Charles St.
Baltimore, MD 21218
alumni@jhu.edu
(410) 516-0363, or
(800) 548-5481

Services Available

The Johns Hopkins University Alumni House is located on Charles Street across the street from the Mattin Center. It is open from 8:30 a.m.–5 p.m. on weekdays during the regular school year. It serves as the headquarters of the alumni association for the eight Johns Hopkins schools, and serves 106,000 alumni from 155 countries. Most students, however, never set foot in the Alumni House because the Alumni Association has placed all of its services online. Students can go to the Alumni House if they want to speak to a representative of the Alumni Association or to buy merchandise.

HopkinsNET is a Web service that allows current students and alumni to search alumni by name, school, geographic region, major, profession, or company name. Thousands of alumni are connected to this service, and can help students learn about possible careers and network.

The Alumni Association sponsors "student send-offs" in over 25 cities, where students can meet students and alumni from their region and learn about life at Hopkins. The Alumni Association also organizes a "Host Family Program," in which students can choose to be matched to a family that will be their family away from home. The host family may take the student to dinner, cultural events, or around Baltimore.

Other benefits to being a paying member of the Alumni Association is that you receive 25 percent discount on Odyssey Program classes, 50 percent off Peabody concerts, 50 percent off admission fees to the historic Homewood and Evergreen houses, 50 percent off ticket prices at Theatre Hopkins, 25 percent discount on books from JHU Press, JHU credit card, up to 10 percent discount on automobile and homeowners' insurance, $240 annual membership to the Recreation Center, Alumni Journeys Travel Program, and membership at the Johns Hopkins Credit Union.

Major Alumni Events

Each of the different schools offers its own Homecoming. The Homecoming for Arts and Science, and Engineering students is held in the spring in conjunction with a lacrosse game. There is a tent party held on one of the quads on Saturday night. Throughout the weekend, the alumni association offers class reunions, campus tours, and socials for departments.

There are 38 regional chapters in the United States and 16 chapters in Europe and Asia. These regional chapters plan between 10 and 20 events per year, from breakfast socials to academic lectures to ballgames to wine tasting.

Alumni Publications

Johns Hopkins Magazine, which is published five times a year, engages a readership of 130,000 readers and keeps them up-to-date on JHU activities, world events, and alumni updates. Yearly subscriptions are 20 dollars within the United States and 24 dollars overseas.

JHUpdate is a monthly e-newsletter that is sent to Hopkins alumni to keep them informed about alumni and university news.

Did You Know?

Famous JHU Alumni:

John Astin (Class of '52) – Actor

John Barth (Class of '51) – Writer

Michael Bloomberg (Class of '64) – New York City Mayor

Wes Craven (Class of '64) –Horror film director

Woodrow Wilson (Class of 1886) – The 28th president of the United States

Student Organizations

Clubs are listed on the Johns Hopkins student organizations Web page, *http://undergraduate.jhu.edu/studentresources/studentorganizations.cfm*

ACLU

Adoramus A Cappella Group

African Student's Association

Agape Campus Ministries, *www.agapechurches.org/campus/jhu.html*

All Nighters A Cappella Group, *www.jhu.edu/~allnight*

Amateur Radio

Amnesty International

Anagram Magazine-Art and Literature of Asian Americans, *www.jhu.edu/~anagram*

Ballroom Dance Club

Barnstormers Theatre Group

Black and Blue Jay Comedy Magazine

Black Student's Union

Buttered Niblets Improv Comedy Group, *www.jhu.edu/~nibs*

Caribbean Cultural Society

Catholic Community (Newman Group)

Chinese Student's Association, *www.jhu.edu/~csa*

Circle K

College Bowl

College Democrats

College Republicans, *www.jhucr.org*

Diverse Sexuality and Gender Alliance (DSAGA), *www.jhu. edu/~dsaga*

Dunbar-Hughes Baldwin Theater Group

Filipino Student's Association, *www.jhu.edu/~fsa*

Gospel Choir, *www.jhu.edu/~gospel*

Habitat for Humanity, *www.jhu.edu/~habitat*

Hellenic Student's Association

Hindu Student's Council

Hong Kong Student's Association

Hopkins's Association for School Spirit

Hopkins's Christian Fellowship (Intervarsity), *www.jhu.edu/~hopcf*

Hopkins's Organization for Pre-Health Education

Hopkins's Science Fiction Association (HOPSFA), *www.jhu. edu/~hopsfa*

Hopkins Symphony Orchestra, *www.jhu.edu/~jhso*

Ice Hockey Club

Indian Cultural Dance Club

Iranian Cultural Society, *www.jhu.edu/ics*

Japanese Student's International, *www.jhu.edu/~jsi*

Jewish Student's Association (HILLEL), *www.jhu.edu/~jsa*

JHU Academic Bowl

JHU Animation Club (JHAC), *www.jhu.edu/~anime*

JHU Association for Computing Machinery

JHU Band

JHU Choral Society

JHU Cycling Club

JHU Math Club

JHU Modern Dance Society

JHU Tennis Club and Club Tennis

JHU Wing Chun Kung Fu Club, *www.jhu.edu/~kclub/index.html*

JMag Literary Magazine

Ketzev A Cappella Group

Korean Student's Association

Ladybirds Dance Group

Mental Notes A Cappella Group, *www.mentalnotes.org*

Middle Eastern Student Affairs

Model United Nations
Muslim Student's Association, *www.jhu.edu/~jhuma*
NAACP
Newsletter, *www.jhunewsletter.com*
Octopodes A Cappella Group, *www.jhu.edu/octopodes*
Organizacion Latina Estudiantil (OLE), *www.jhu.edu/~ole*
Outdoors Club, *www.jhu.edu/~outdoors*
Pre-Law Society
Public Health Student Forum, *www.jhu.edu/phsf*
Pugwash
Sirens A Cappella, *http://jhuniverse.hcf.jhu.edu/~sirens*
Soo-Bahk Do Club
South Asian Student's Association
Stepping Stones
Student Council
Students for Choice
Students for Environmental Action, *www.jhu.edu/~sea*
Students for a Free Tibet
Table Tennis
TaeKwonDo, *www.jhu.edu/~tclub*
TASA
Turkish Student's Association
Ultimate Frisbee Club
Vietnamese Student's Association
Vocal Chords A Cappella Group, *www.jhu.edu/~vchords*
Witness Theater
Zeniada Literary Magazine

The Best
& Worst

The Ten BEST Things About JHU

1 Research opportunities abound. If you want to do research as an undergraduate, Hopkins is a great choice.

2 Hopkins has a beautiful, green campus.

3 Students organize symposia and lectures with world-class speakers. These speakers discuss topics from engineering to international relations to film.

4 Baltimore City is a great mid-size city that offers many entertainment options. Washington, DC is an easy day-trip away.

5 You can walk anywhere on campus and to almost all off-campus housing within 15 minutes.

6 Off-campus housing is affordable. Baltimore is a city with a low cost of living.

7 Off-campus dining at area restaurants is convenient and affordable. Baltimore, and even Charles Village, has a varied selection of American and ethnic foods.

8 Students love the name recognition that follows after telling someone that they attend Johns Hopkins. It helps students network successfully and find jobs.

9 One of the best things about Hopkins academically is the unity within departments. Small departments like biophysics, classics, and mechanical engineering are known for close friendships between students and faculty mentors.

10 Hopkins lacks a general core curriculum for all students. Individual majors have requirements, but there are no courses that everyone takes. Because of this, students are able to choose which courses they want to take when they have extra space in their schedules.

The Ten **WORST** Things About JHU

1 Many students feel that professors are more concerned with their own research than with helping the students they teach.

2 Even with all of the effort that the administration has put into landscaping and remodeling buildings, Hopkins always seems like it's under construction.

3 Hopkins lacks traditional school spirit. Students are proud of the Hopkins name and reputation, but not its athletics.

4 Baltimore City is a small city with nothing to do. Hopkins isn't even part of the downtown area.

5 There are unsafe neighborhoods surrounding Hopkins, and new students need to learn where they should and should not walk.

6 When students live off campus junior and senior year, they have to work to create their own social lives. If they aren't willing to look for things to do, they'll end up bored.

7 The on-campus meal plan leaves lots to be desired. Although there's a wide selection of foods offered, students dislike the meal plan requirement for freshmen and sophomores. It is expensive, and the dining halls repeat food choices often.

8 With the name recognition attached, especially to the medical school, students expect to have an adequate health and wellness center. The Student Health and Wellness Center, however, is famous around campus for misdiagnosing student illnesses. Even when illnesses are easily diagnosed with tests, the center has denied giving these tests or medications unless students insist on it.

9 Unity among students is undermined by competitive cutthroat students. These students are entirely focused on their studies and will sabotage the work of other students who might hinder their progression towards medical school.

10 Although the Career Center works well with students who actually follow its advice and meet with career counselors all four years, it is less prepared to deal with students who wait until senior year to meet with career counselors and those students who are unsure about what they want to do with their lives. Students complain that the Career Center doesn't listen to what students say they want to do, but instead tries to push all students along similar paths.

Visiting

The Lowdown On...
Visiting

Hotel Information:

Homewood Area:
(within one mile from campus)

Doubletree Inn at the Colonnade
4 W University Pkwy.
Baltimore, MD 21210
(410) 235-5400
(800) 222-TREE
Price Range: $135–$160

Hopkins Inn
3404 St. Paul St.
Baltimore, MD 21218
(410) 235-8600
Price Range: $100–$150

Quality Inn Suites at the Carlyle
500 W University Pkwy.
Baltimore, MD 21210
(410) 889-4500
(800) 424-6423
Fax: 410-467-3073
Price Range: $90–$150

→

Inner Harbor Area:
(within one to five miles
from campus)

Admiral Fell Inn
888 S Broadway
Baltimore, MD 21231
(410) 522-7377
Price Range: $150

Baltimore Marriott
Inner Harbor
110 South Eutaw St.
Baltimore, MD 21201
(410) 962-0202
(800) 228-9290
Price Range: $230–$280

Biltmore Suites
205 W Madison St.
Baltimore, MD 21201
(410) 728-6550
(800) 868-5064
Price Range: $120–$150

Clarion Hotel Peabody Court
612 Cathedral St.
Baltimore, MD 21201
(410) 727-7101
(800) 292-5500
Price Range: $130–$160

Days Inn Baltimore
Inner Harbor
100 Hopkins Pl.
Baltimore, MD 21201
(410) 576-1000
(800) 329-7466
Price Range: $100

Harbor Court Hotel
550 Light St.
Baltimore, MD 21202
(410) 234-0550
Price Range: $205–$240

Holiday Inn Inner Harbor
301 W Lombard St.
Baltimore, MD 21201
(410) 685-3500
(800) HOLIDAY
Fax: (410) 727-6169
Price Range: $120–$145

Hyatt Regency Baltimore
300 Light St.
Baltimore, MD 21202
(410) 528-1234
(800) 233-1234
Price Range: $270–$320

Inn at Henderson's Wharf
1000 Fell St.
Baltimore, MD 21231
(410) 522-7777
(800) 522-2088
Price Range: $180–$210

Pier 5 Hotel (next to National Aquarium)
711 Eastern Ave.
Baltimore, MD 21202
(410) 539-2000
Price Range: $240–$300

Mt. Vernon Hotel
24 W Franklin St.
Baltimore, MD 21201
(410) 727-2000,
(800) 245-5256
Price Range: $100–$120

**Radisson Plaza Lord
Baltimore Hotel**
20-30 W Baltimore St.
Baltimore, MD 21201
(410) 539-8400
Price Range: $90–$140

**Renaissance Harborplace
Hotel**
202 E Pratt St.
Baltimore, MD 21202
(410) 547-1200
Fax: (410) 539-5780
Price Range: $170–$235

Sheraton Inner Harbor Hotel
300 S Charles St.
Baltimore, MD 21201
(410) 962-8300
Price Range: $135–$200

Tremont Suite Hotels
222 St. Paul Pl.
Baltimore, MD 21202
(410) 727-2222
Price Range: $105–$135

**Wyndham Baltimore
Inner Harbor Hotel**
101 W Fayette St.
Baltimore, MD 21201
(410) 752-1100
Price Range: $92

Take a Campus Virtual Tour

http://apply.jhu.edu/visit/tour.html

To Schedule a Group Information Session or Interview

Call (410) 516-8171 between 9 a.m. to 3 p.m. Monday to Friday. The office encourages two weeks advance notice when scheduling an interview. Due to a high volume of requests, however, they cannot always guarantee availability. Interviews are offered weekdays in the Office of Undergraduate Admissions, 140 Garland Hall for juniors in high school. Seniors applying regular decision may request an alumni interview through Monday, January 6th by calling (410) 516-8171.

Campus Tours

Any visitor may participate in a guided tour of campus leaving from Garland Hall Monday–Friday. Reservations are only required if your group has 20 or more people. Groups of 20 or more must call out office at (410) 516-8171 at least two weeks in advance to make special arrangements for a guided tour. During the summer, tours leave at 10 a.m. and 1 p.m. They are generally offered every hour on the hour between 9 a.m. and 4 p.m. during the school year. On selected Saturdays throughout the summer and fall, Hopkins offers a two-hour program starting at 11 a.m. that includes an information session and a guided tour of the campus. Reservations are required for the Saturday programs. Call the 24-hour RSVP line at (410) 516-6881 to reserve your spot. The program begins at the Admissions Office at 140 Garland Hall at 11 a.m. If there are no walking tours when you are coming, try the self-guided walking tour. You can pick up your guide from Admissions during office hours Monday to Friday 9 a.m.–4:30 p.m., or on weekends from the Security Office in Shriver Hall.

Overnight Visits

Visits are encouraged for prospective and current applicants during the fall, and accepted applicants during the spring. Students can visit selected Sunday evenings and weeknights during fall and spring semesters, and selected dates in conjunction with on-campus programs. To schedule a date, visit the Hopkins Hosting Society Web site at *http://apply.jhu. edu/visit/hopkinshosting.html* or contact by phone at (410) 516-2379 at least two weeks in advance. No overnights will be offered during the following times: reading period; finals; winter, spring, and summer breaks; and Orientation.

Directions to Campus

Driving from the North

From I-95 Southbound or I-695 (Baltimore Beltway), get on the beltway and take it toward Towson to exit 25. Take Charles Street south for about seven miles (when Charles Street splits a block after Loyola College and Cold Spring Lane, take the right fork). As you approach the University and cross University Parkway, continue southbound, but be sure to jog right onto the service road. After you pass the University on the right, turn right onto Art Museum Drive. Just after the Baltimore Museum of Art, bear right at the traffic island onto Wyman Park Drive. Take an almost immediate right through the University gates. A visitors lot and parking meters will be on the left.

Driving from the South

From I-95 Southbound, take exit 53 onto I-395 North toward downtown Baltimore, then take the exit to Martin Luther King Jr. Boulevard. Take King Boulevard north until it ends at Howard Street (remain in one of the middle lanes of King Boulevard to avoid a premature forced right or left turn). Turn left at Howard Street, and proceed about two miles. One block past 29th Street, turn left at the traffic island (just before the Baltimore Museum of Art) onto Wyman Park Drive. Take an almost immediate right through the University gates. A visitors lot and parking meters will be on the left.

Driving from the East

Drive to I-695 (Baltimore beltway) or I-95 and follow directions above.

Driving from the West

Drive to I-695 (Baltimore beltway) or I-95 and follow directions above.

Words to Know

Academic Probation – A suspension imposed on a student if he or she fails to keep up with the school's minimum academic requirements. Those unable to improve their grades after receiving this warning can face dismissal.

Beer Pong/Beirut – A drinking game involving cups of beer arranged in a pyramid shape on each side of a table. The goal is to get a ping pong ball into one of the opponent's cups by throwing the ball or hitting it with a paddle. If the ball lands in a cup, the opponent is required to drink the beer.

Bid – An invitation from a fraternity or sorority to 'pledge' (join) that specific house.

Blue-Light Phone – Brightly-colored phone posts with a blue light bulb on top. These phones exist for security purposes and are located at various outside locations around most campuses. In an emergency, a student can pick up one of these phones (free of charge) to connect with campus police or a security escort.

Campus Police – Police who are specifically assigned to a given institution. Campus police are typically not regular city officers; they are employed by the university in a full-time capacity.

Club Sports – A level of sports that falls somewhere between varsity and intramural. If a student is unable to commit to a varsity team but has a lot of passion for athletics, a club sport could be a better, less intense option. Even less demanding, intramural (IM) sports often involve no traveling and considerably less time.

Cocaine – An illegal drug. Also known as "coke" or "blow," cocaine often resembles a white crystalline or powdery substance. It is highly addictive and dangerous.

Common Application – An application with which students can apply to multiple schools.

Course Registration – The period of official class selection for the upcoming quarter or semester. Prior to registration, it is best to prepare several back-up courses in case a particular class becomes full. If a course is full, students can place themselves on the waitlist, although this still does not guarantee entry.

Division Athletics – Athletic classifications range from Division I to Division III. Division IA is the most competitive, while Division III is considered to be the least competitive.

Dorm – A dorm (or dormitory) is an on-campus housing facility. Dorms can provide a range of options from suite-style rooms to more communal options that include shared bathrooms. Most first-year students live in dorms. Some upperclassmen who wish to stay on campus also choose this option.

Early Action – An application option with which a student can apply to a school and receive an early acceptance response without a binding commitment. This system is becoming less and less available.

Early Decision – An application option that students should use only if they are certain they plan to attend the school in question. If a student applies using the early decision option and is admitted, he or she is required and bound to attend that university. Admission rates are usually higher among students who apply through early decision, as the student is clearly indicating that the school is his or her first choice.

Ecstasy – An illegal drug. Also known as "E" or "X," ecstasy looks like a pill and most resembles an aspirin. Considered a party drug, ecstasy is very dangerous and can be deadly.

Ethernet – An extremely fast Internet connection available in most university-owned residence halls. To use an Ethernet connection properly, a student will need a network card and cable for his or her computer.

Fake ID – A counterfeit identification card that contains false information. Most commonly, students get fake IDs with altered birthdates so that they appear to be older than 21 (and therefore of legal drinking age). Even though it is illegal, many college students have fake IDs in hopes of purchasing alcohol or getting into bars.

Frosh – Slang for "freshman" or "freshmen."

Hazing – Initiation rituals administered by some fraternities or sororities as part of the pledging process. Many universities have outlawed hazing due to its degrading, and sometimes dangerous, nature.

Intramurals (IMs) – A popular, and usually free, sport league in which students create teams and compete against one another. These sports vary in competitiveness and can include a range of activities—everything from billiards to water polo. IM sports are a great way to meet people with similar interests.

Keg – Officially called a half-barrel, a keg contains roughly 200 12-ounce servings of beer.

LSD – An illegal drug, also known as acid, this hallucinogenic drug most commonly resembles a tab of paper.

Marijuana – An illegal drug, also known as weed or pot; along with alcohol, marijuana is one of the most commonly-found drugs on campuses across the country.

Major –The focal point of a student's college studies; a specific topic that is studied for a degree. Examples of majors include physics, English, history, computer science, economics, business, and music. Many students decide on a specific major before arriving on campus, while others are simply "undecided" until declaring a major. Those who are extremely interested in two areas can also choose to double major.

Meal Block – The equivalent of one meal. Students on a meal plan usually receive a fixed number of meals per week. Each meal, or "block," can be redeemed at the school's dining facilities in place of cash. Often, a student's weekly allotment of meal blocks will be forfeited if not used.

Minor – An additional focal point in a student's education. Often serving as a complement or addition to a student's main area of focus, a minor has fewer requirements and prerequisites to fulfill than a major. Minors are not required for graduation from most schools; however some students who want to explore many different interests choose to pursue both a major and a minor.

Mushrooms – An illegal drug. Also known as "'shrooms," this drug resembles regular mushrooms but is extremely hallucinogenic.

Off-Campus Housing – Housing from a particular landlord or rental group that is not affiliated with the university. Depending on the college, off-campus housing can range from extremely popular to non-existent. Students who choose to live off campus are typically given more freedom, but they also have to deal with possible subletting scenarios, furniture, bills, and other issues. In addition to these factors, rental prices and distance often affect a student's decision to move off campus.

Office Hours – Time that teachers set aside for students who have questions about coursework. Office hours are a good forum for students to go over any problems and to show interest in the subject material.

Pledging – The early phase of joining a fraternity or sorority, pledging takes place after a student has gone through rush and received a bid. Pledging usually lasts between one and two semesters. Once the pledging period is complete and a particular student has done everything that is required to become a member, that student is considered a brother or sister. If a fraternity or a sorority would decide to "haze" a group of students, this initiation would take place during the pledging period.

Private Institution – A school that does not use tax revenue to subsidize education costs. Private schools typically cost more than public schools and are usually smaller.

Prof – Slang for "professor."

Public Institution – A school that uses tax revenue to subsidize education costs. Public schools are often a good value for in-state residents and tend to be larger than most private colleges.

Quarter System (or Trimester System) – A type of academic calendar system. In this setup, students take classes for three academic periods. The first quarter usually starts in late September or early October and concludes right before Christmas. The second quarter usually starts around early to mid–January and finishes up around March or April. The last academic quarter, or "third quarter," usually starts in late March or early April and finishes up in late May or Mid-June. The fourth quarter is summer. The major difference between the quarter system and semester system is that students take more, less comprehensive courses under the quarter calendar.

RA (Resident Assistant) – A student leader who is assigned to a particular floor in a dormitory in order to help to the other students who live there. An RA's duties include ensuring student safety and providing assistance wherever possible.

Recitation – An extension of a specific course; a review session. Some classes, particularly large lectures, are supplemented with mandatory recitation sessions that provide a relatively personal class setting.

Rolling Admissions – A form of admissions. Most commonly found at public institutions, schools with this type of policy continue to accept students throughout the year until their class sizes are met. For example, some schools begin accepting students as early as December and will continue to do so until April or May.

Room and Board – This figure is typically the combined cost of a university-owned room and a meal plan.

Room Draw/Housing Lottery – A common way to pick on-campus room assignments for the following year. If a student decides to remain in university-owned housing, he or she is assigned a unique number that, along with seniority, is used to determine his or her housing for the next year.

Rush – The period in which students can meet the brothers and sisters of a particular chapter and find out if a given fraternity or sorority is right for them. Rushing a fraternity or a sorority is not a requirement at any school. The goal of rush is to give students who are serious about pledging a feel for what to expect.

Semester System – The most common type of academic calendar system at college campuses. This setup typically includes two semesters in a given school year. The fall semester starts around the end of August or early September and concludes before winter vacation. The spring semester usually starts in mid-January and ends in late April or May.

Student Center/Rec Center/Student Union – A common area on campus that often contains study areas, recreation facilities, and eateries. This building is often a good place to meet up with fellow students; depending on the school, the student center can have a huge role or a non-existent role in campus life.

Student ID – A university-issued photo ID that serves as a student's key to school-related functions. Some schools require students to show these cards in order to get into dorms, libraries, cafeterias, and other facilities. In addition to storing meal plan information, in some cases, a student ID can actually work as a debit card and allow students to purchase things from bookstores or local shops.

Suite – A type of dorm room. Unlike dorms that feature communal bathrooms shared by the entire floor, suites offer bathrooms shared only among the suite. Suite-style dorm rooms can house anywhere from two to ten students.

TA (Teacher's Assistant) – An undergraduate or grad student who helps in some manner with a specific course. In some cases, a TA will teach a class, assist a professor, grade assignments, or conduct office hours.

Undergraduate – A student in the process of studying for his or her bachelor's degree.

ABOUT THE AUTHOR

I hope this book has told you more about Hopkins than you've learned from all of the promotional material Hopkins has sent to you. I learned a lot about Hopkins when researching the material for this book. Much of it would have been of use during the past four years, but it's better late than never! I graduated from Hopkins with a double major in political science and writing seminars. While I had a great experience at Hopkins, it isn't the school for everyone. I hope that this book will help you decide if Hopkins is the school for you. Don't, however, rely too heavily on it. Information changes quickly, and much of the feel of the freshman class is decided by the freshman themselves. A book can't tell you what Hopkins will be like for you, just what it has been like for other people. Make the most of your college experience. If you have any questions or comments, please contact me by e-mail.

I would like to thank many people for their help, especially Seth, Mom, Dad, College Prowler, and all of the Hopkins students who took the time to tell me about their experience at Hopkins.

Christina Pommer
christinapommer@collegeprowler.com

The College Prowler Big Book of Colleges

Having Trouble Narrowing Down Your Choices?

Try Going Bigger!

BIG BOOK OF COLLEGES '09
7¼" X 10", 1248 Pages Paperback
$29.95 Retail
978-1-4274-0005-5

Choosing the perfect school can be an overwhelming challenge. Luckily, our *Big Book of Colleges* makes that task a little less daunting. We've packed it with overviews of our full library of single-school guides—more than 280 of the nation's top schools—giving you some much-needed perspective on your search.

College Prowler on the Web

Craving some electronic interaction? Check out the new and improved **CollegeProwler.com**! We've included the COMPLETE contents of more than 250 of our single-school guides on the Web—and you can gain access to all of them for just $39.95 per year!

Not only that, but non-subscribers can still view and compare our grades for each school, order books at our online bookstore, or enter our monthly scholarship contest. Don't get left in the dark when making your college decision. Let College Prowler be your guide!

Get the Jolt!

College Jolt gives you a peek behind the scenes

College Jolt is our new blog designed to hook you up with great information, funny videos, cool contests, awesome scholarship opportunities, and honest insight into who we are and what we're all about.

Check us out at ***www.collegejolt.com***

Tell Us What Life Is Really Like at Your School!

Have you ever wanted to let people know what your college is really like? Now's your chance to help millions of high school students choose the right college.

Let your voice be heard.

Check out **www.collegeprowler.com** for more info!

Need More Help?

Do you have more questions about this school? Can't find a certain statistic? College Prowler is here to help. We are the best source of college information out there. We have a network of thousands of students who can get the latest information on any school to you ASAP. E-mail us at info@collegeprowler.com with your college-related questions.

E-Mail Us Your College-Related Questions!

Check out *www.collegeprowler.com* for more details.
1-800-290-2682

Write For Us!
Get published! Voice your opinion.

Writing a College Prowler guidebook is both fun and rewarding; our open-ended format allows your own creativity free reign. Our writers have been featured in national newspapers and have seen their names in bookstores across the country. Now is your chance to break into the publishing industry with one of the country's fastest-growing publishers!

Apply now at ***www.collegeprowler.com***

Contact editor@collegeprowler.com or call 1-800-290-2682 for more details.

Pros and Cons

Still can't figure out if this is the right school for you?
You've already read through this in-depth guide;
why not list the pros and cons? It will really help
with narrowing down your decision and determining
whether or not this school is right for you.

Pros	Cons
....	....
....	....
....	....
....	....
....	....
....	....
....	....
....	....
....	....
....	....
....	....
....	....
....	....

Pros and Cons

Still can't figure out if this is the right school for you?
You've already read through this in-depth guide;
why not list the pros and cons? It will really help
with narrowing down your decision and determining
whether or not this school is right for you.

Pros	Cons
....	....
....	....
....	....
....	....
....	....
....	....
....	....
....	....
....	....
....	....
....	....
....	....
....	....

Notes

Notes

....

....

....

....

....

....

....

....

....

....

....

....

....

Notes

....

....

....

....

....

....

....

....

....

....

....

....

....

Notes

....

....

....

....

....

....

....

....

....

....

....

....

....

Notes

....

....

....

....

....

....

....

....

....

....

....

....

....

Notes

....

....

....

....

....

....

....

....

....

....

....

....

....

Notes

....

....

....

....

....

....

....

....

....

....

....

....

....

Notes

Notes

....

....

....

....

....

....

....

....

....

....

....

....

....

Notes

Notes

....

....

....

....

....

....

....

....

....

....

....

....

....

Notes

....

....

....

....

....

....

....

....

....

....

....

....

....

Notes

....

....

....

....

....

....

....

....

....

....

....

....

....

Notes

....

....

....

....

....

....

....

....

....

....

....

....

....

....

Notes

....

....

....

....

....

....

....

....

....

....

....

....

....

Albion College
Alfred University
Allegheny College
American University
Amherst College
Arizona State University
Auburn University
Babson College
Ball State University
Bard College
Barnard College
Bates College
Baylor University
Beloit College
Bentley College
Binghamton University
Birmingham Southern College
Boston College
Boston University
Bowdoin College
Brandeis University
Brigham Young University
Brown University
Bryn Mawr College
Bucknell University
Cal Poly
Cal Poly Pomona
Cal State Northridge
Cal State Sacramento
Caltech
Carleton College
Carnegie Mellon University
Case Western Reserve
Centenary College of Louisiana
Centre College
Claremont McKenna College
Clark Atlanta University
Clark University
Clemson University
Colby College
Colgate University
College of Charleston
College of the Holy Cross
College of William & Mary
College of Wooster
Colorado College
Columbia University
Connecticut College
Cornell University
Creighton University
CUNY Hunters College
Dartmouth College
Davidson College
Denison University
DePauw University
Dickinson College
Drexel University
Duke University
Duquesne University
Earlham College
East Carolina University
Elon University
Emerson University
Emory University
FIT
Florida State University
Fordham University

Franklin & Marshall College
Furman University
Geneva College
George Washington University
Georgetown University
Georgia Tech
Gettysburg College
Gonzaga University
Goucher College
Grinnell College
Grove City College
Guilford College
Gustavus Adolphus College
Hamilton College
Hampshire College
Hampton University
Hanover College
Harvard University
Harvey Mudd College
Haverford College
Hofstra University
Hollins University
Howard University
Idaho State University
Illinois State University
Illinois Wesleyan University
Indiana University
Iowa State University
Ithaca College
IUPUI
James Madison University
Johns Hopkins University
Juniata College
Kansas State
Kent State University
Kenyon College
Lafayette College
LaRoche College
Lawrence University
Lehigh University
Lewis & Clark College
Louisiana State University
Loyola College in Maryland
Loyola Marymount University
Loyola University Chicago
Loyola University New Orleans
Macalester College
Marlboro College
Marquette University
McGill University
Miami University of Ohio
Michigan State University
Middle Tennessee State
Middlebury College
Millsaps College
MIT
Montana State University
Mount Holyoke College
Muhlenberg College
New York University
North Carolina State
Northeastern University
Northern Arizona University
Northern Illinois University
Northwestern University
Oberlin College
Occidental College

Ohio State University
Ohio University
Ohio Wesleyan University
Old Dominion University
Penn State University
Pepperdine University
Pitzer College
Pomona College
Princeton University
Providence College
Purdue University
Reed College
Rensselaer Polytechnic Institute
Rhode Island School of Design
Rhodes College
Rice University
Rochester Institute of Technology
Rollins College
Rutgers University
San Diego State University
Santa Clara University
Sarah Lawrence College
Scripps College
Seattle University
Seton Hall University
Simmons College
Skidmore College
Slippery Rock
Smith College
Southern Methodist University
Southwestern University
Spelman College
St. Joseph's University Philladelphia
St. John's University
St. Louis University
St. Olaf College
Stanford University
Stetson University
Stony Brook University
Susquahanna University
Swarthmore College
Syracuse University
Temple University
Tennessee State University
Texas A & M University
Texas Christian University
Towson University
Trinity College Connecticut
Trinity University Texas
Truman State
Tufts University
Tulane University
UC Berkeley
UC Davis
UC Irvine
UC Riverside
UC San Diego
UC Santa Barbara
UC Santa Cruz
UCLA
Union College
University at Albany
University at Buffalo
University of Alabama
University of Arizona
University of Central Florida
University of Chicago

University of Colorado
University of Connecticut
University of Delaware
University of Denver
University of Florida
University of Georgia
University of Illinois
University of Iowa
University of Kansas
University of Kentucky
University of Maine
University of Maryland
University of Massachusetts
University of Miami
University of Michigan
University of Minnesota
University of Mississippi
University of Missouri
University of Nebraska
University of New Hampshire
University of North Carolina
University of Notre Dame
University of Oklahoma
University of Oregon
University of Pennsylvania
University of Pittsburgh
University of Puget Sound
University of Rhode Island
University of Richmond
University of Rochester
University of San Diego
University of San Francisco
University of South Carolina
University of South Dakota
University of South Florida
University of Southern California
University of Tennessee
University of Texas
University of Utah
University of Vermont
University of Virginia
University of Washington
University of Wisconsin
UNLV
Ursinus College
Valparaiso University
Vanderbilt University
Vassar College
Villanova University
Virginia Tech
Wake Forest University
Warren Wilson College
Washington and Lee University
Washington University in St. Louis
Wellesley College
Wesleyan University
West Point
West Virginia University
Wheaton College IL
Wheaton College MA
Whitman College
Wilkes University
Williams College
Xavier University
Yale University

Printed in the United States
220439BV00004B/2/P

9 781427 400826